D1713517

HYMNAL HANDBOOK

FOR

Standard Hymns

AND

Gospel Songs

AMS PRESS
NEW YORK

HYMNAL HANDBOOK
FOR
Standard Hymns
AND
Gospel Songs

A collection of stories and information about Hymns, Gospel
songs and their writers, designed to help ministers
and music directors create greater appreciation
and interest in congregational singing.

BY

HOMER A. RODEHEAVER

THE RODEHEAVER COMPANY

CHICAGO
28 E. Jackson Boulevard

PHILADELPHIA
721 Arch Street

Library of Congress Cataloging in Publication Data

Rodeheaver, Homer Alvan, 1880-1955.
   Hymnal handbook for Standard hymns and gospel
songs.

   Reprint of the 1931 ed. published by Rodeheaver
Co., Chicago.
   1. Hymns, English—History and criticism.
I. Standard church hymns and gospel songs. II. Title.
ML3186.R68   1975   783.9   72-1686
ISBN 0-404-09913-0

From the edition of 1931, Chicago and Philadelphia
First AMS edition published in 1975
Manufactured in the United States of America

AMS PRESS INC.
NEW YORK, N. Y. 10003

Introduction

You meet individuals on a street or in a crowd and they mean nothing. But when you are introduced and learn something of their parentage, birthplace, personal interest and problems, you find new pleasure and profit through new friends. So, we want to introduce you and have you become friends of STANDARD HYMNS AND GOSPEL SONGS by telling you interesting facts of their origin, of the men and women who have written them, and of some of the great blessings they have brought to other folks, that you may use these facts to make a real blessing to many others, and give them a new interest in this kind of music.

All of us who have conducted song services, and most of us who have listened, realize how much more interest we have in a song when we know something personal about it. We also realize how difficult it is to find these facts and stories.

So, with the hope that I may help all of you to make your song services more interesting and more helpful, I am giving you in this book some facts and stories about the songs and authors represented in STANDARD HYMNS AND GOSPEL SONGS. Ministers and music directors, using this song book in church or Sunday school, can turn to the corresponding number in this handbook and find authentic facts and information.

To Julian's *Dictionary of Hymnology,* the standard authority on hymns in English, I am indebted for many facts and incidents recorded in this book. To those authors of hymns and composers of tunes who have responded graciously to my requests for information about their own productions, I am deeply grateful; to my good friends, George W. Sanville, for incidents from his memory and experiences which he has contributed, and especially Carl F. Price, who has given very valuable help in suggesting the best sources of hymnological facts and information.

About some of the hymns and songs we do not have any especially interesting stories; but we have given authors and dates as authentically as possible. The cross-reference plan will enable you to follow through and easily find these facts about the authors and their songs.

Homer Rodeheaver

Suggestions for the Song Leader

MUSIC is the universal language of the human soul. It touches the entire scale of human emotions. Inspired by its stirring rhythm and influence, men forget fear and rush into battle to kill and destroy, while with its soft cadences and melody, gentle mothers lull little babies to sleep. In our church life, it is the one medium through which we can all get together, regardless of creed or denomination. Churches, that would not interchange pulpits, sing hymns written by leaders of other denominations, and find great and helpful spiritual ideas and facts that are common to all. Music, if made sufficiently attractive, interesting and helpful, is the field of religious activity and worship where the greatest number can participate; thus helping to solve one of the greatest problems of the church, that of giving the membership a personal, active part.

What is the difference between a hymn and a gospel song? Have you ever considered this question? This definition will not apply in every instance, but, as a general rule, the hymn is addressed to God in prayer, praise, adoration or worship. The gospel song is addressed to people, presenting some phase of God's plan of salvation as outlined in the gospel, with admonition, warning, testimony and expressions of joy because of salvation. With this definition before us, there should be no controversy as to the use of hymns and gospel songs; we can readily see there is a great need for both. I hope we all want to praise and worship through the great hymns, and also have a desire that God's plan of salvation should be given to people through the gospel songs.

We must remember that some gospel songs are for a specific purpose, outside of the formal service of the church, and they meet the musical and literary understanding of a big majority of folks not trained in the classics. They do understand and appreciate simple, direct statements, blended with easy rhythm and beautiful melody, and they would not care for great, majestic harmonies, nor understand the theological terms of some of the great hymns.

We appreciate the importance of a certain amount of formality and dignity in the Sunday morning service, but some of these suggestions might even be helpful there, although we are thinking specifically of the other general song services of the church, the Sunday school, Young People's meetings, and Sunday night services.

Have you ever been in a service where all the hymns were unfamiliar and you did not enjoy it because you could not take part? Some of the folks are like you. I was in a large church not long ago where all the hymns were so difficult and unfamiliar that in a very large audience I could see only six people who even tried to sing. The choir and the organ carried the service on, but the people missed the blessing they should have had through participation. The hymns may have been carefully selected and their literary content may have been perfect for the sermon, but I wonder if a happy medium in the selection of at least a few familiar hymns would not have helped the service.

Yes, there is the great danger of singing over and over a few familiar hymns, and not learning the new ones, but this can be avoided by gradually introducing the new ones and by setting aside a special period for study and rehearsal of new hymns. This has been done on prayer meeting nights, thus increasing the interest there. Also a part of the Sunday night song service could be given to learning new or unfamiliar hymns.

In a song service of thirty minutes, I would not introduce more than one or two entirely new hymns. Nor would I spend too much time on any one new hymn, but try it over, teach it to the folks, and then go ahead with the regular song service, and the next time take it up again, until very soon it becomes a familiar hymn.

The preacher or leader of any service should have a conference with the director of music, outlining the general theme and purpose of the meeting. Then, the music can be selected that will create the right atmosphere for that particular service. The selection of the hymns is even more important than the singing or directing. Well selected hymns with poor directing will help a service more than poorly selected hymns with good directing.

Thinking now of the general song service; for an opening song we would select a song that is within itself a real prayer for a song service. These numbers I give, refer to the songs in STANDARD HYMNS AND GOSPEL SONGS: No. 9. "Come, Thou Almighty King." Notice particularly how this hymn is divided, referring first to the "Almighty King," then to the "Incarnate Word," and then to the "Holy Comforter," and finally summing it all up in the last stanza, "To the great One in Three, Eternal praises be." A splendid effect can be gotten from this song by singing the third stanza very softly. No. 1. "O worship the King." No. 8. "O for a thousand tongues to sing." For the morning service, especially, No. 39. "Holy, holy, holy, Lord God Almighty, Early in the morning our songs shall rise to Thee."

Suppose the theme is Christian leadership, with Jesus as the example. After the opening prayer song, magnify and adore the name of Jesus with No. 52, "Fairest Lord Jesus." Then call upon all the people to praise His name with No. 78, "All hail the power of Jesus' Name." Then, acknowledge personal and individual love and loyalty with No. 311, "My Jesus, I love Thee, I know Thou art mine." One or two stanzas of this could be sung as a duet. Then, after praising His name and acknowledging our personal love and loyalty, use the great martial hymn, No. 138, "Lead on, O King Eternal," and No. 147, "O ye, who dare go forth with God," No. 146, "Soldiers of the cross, arise!" Then, if there is an appeal, a great closing song would be No. 298, "Where He Leads me I will Follow."

When you are selecting these programs, turn to the corresponding number in this Hand Book, where you will find interesting facts about each song, which will make your song service more interesting. It is not necessary to give facts in your song service about each song, but it is tremendously helpful to have some interesting facts about some of the songs.

Suppose the subject for the meeting is "The Cross." A splendid opening song would be No. 71, "When I survey the wondrous cross." Follow this with No. 69, "In the cross of Christ I glory, Tow'ring o'er the wrecks of time," and then let someone sing as a solo or duet No. 324, "The Old Rugged Cross."

A very striking way to use "The Old Rugged Cross" is to let someone sing the stanza as a solo or duet, and let the choir immediately follow at the end of the first chorus with the first stanza of "Must Jesus bear the cross alone, And all the world go free." Then, after the last stanza, let the choir sing

> "The consecrated cross I'll bear,
>   Till death shall set me free,
> And then go home my crown to wear,
>   For there's a crown for me."

For special days, special seasons and special subjects, you will find a splendid and complete topical index in the front part of STANDARD HYMNS AND GOSPEL SONGS. These suggestions, of course, should be used as a guide, because every service should have a certain individuality. If you do not know in advance how the sermon is going to close, but you do know you will be called upon for a congregational song or a solo, you should follow the sermon through very carefully. As different suitable songs are suggested, slip a little piece of paper in the book where that song is located, or put one finger in there. As the sermon proceeds, another will be suggested. The theme may change, naturally eliminating some song that you have selected, but if this is carefully done, when the preacher comes to the close of his sermon and turns to you and asks for a song, you will have one of the very best songs in the book ready to sing immediately. If you should not do this, and the preacher should call on you for a song, and you would have to turn back to the topical index, find a suitable song, and then have a pianist play the prelude for you, by the time you got to it, it would be too late for the song to be especially effective. An unnecessary pause and delay would spoil to a certain extent the spirit of the service.

Especially important is the selection of the invitation song. If the invitation is a challenge to men and women, an appeal to their courage, the invitation song could be No. 148, "Stand up for Jesus," or No. 144, "Onward, Christian soldiers," or No. 299, "Rescue the perishing." If the invitation is in the form of a tender appeal, then, of course, you should select No. 102, "Just as I am," or No. 365, "Almost persuaded," or No. 356, "Softly and tenderly Jesus is calling." If the appeal should be particularly to the church, to rededicate or reconsecrate their lives for definite service, then you could use No. 294, "I'm pressing on the upward way," or No. 302, "I'll go where You want me to go."

One very interesting way to create interest in a song service is to divide your audience in sections and let them sing antiphonally. For instance, if you have people in a gallery or a Sunday school room, sing a song like "For you I am praying." After you have gone through it once, let your choir sing the first phrase of the chorus, the people in the gallery or Sunday school room the second phrase, your choir the third phrase, and this other crowd the last. Another song that can be used effectively this way is "Let the lower lights be burning!" Another is "Where He leads me I will follow." This is also a splendid way to use your children without long, strenuous rehearsals. Let the children occupy a section in the gallery or the Sunday school room and use them as the antiphonal chorus on some of these simple songs. You can also divide the men and women on phrases of this kind, letting the men sing one phrase and the women the other.

Now for some practical suggestions: Here are a few suggestions for the actual direction of the music. First of all, see that the piano is placed so that the accompanist can easily see the director. How many of you know churches where the pianist has to sit with his back to the director? As the director, see that your platform is high enough so that people can easily see you. See in advance that all the folks have books. Announce the number two or three times so that all will hear.

The direction should be done modestly, and in proportion to the size of the crowd; of course, remembering that the larger the crowd, the greater must be the movement of your hands, and with either the large or small crowd, the direction should be very clear, particularly marking the accents with a downward beat of the hand.

With the hand, mark the accents, the beginning and the holds, and the finish of the stanzas so no one can misunderstand. Remember that most folks want to sing. The chief reason for not singing is fear of making a mistake. Remember also that a very small proportion of the people in the average audience actually read music. With clear, plain movements of your hands, you give them the musical education they have been unable to acquire, tempo, rhythm, note and rest value. Mark your beats so clearly and distinctly that they cannot be mistaken. Encourage folks with a smile and as much praise as possible. Point out their mistakes and make suggestions as a friend, and not as a musical critic.

The introduction of a story, that is interesting and that really illustrates a point, is a splendid feature, but you must be very careful not to overdo this. A good stock of stories is exceedingly valuable to any man before the public, and especially a song leader or master of ceremonies, if he knows how to use them. Many times it will save an embarrassing situation.

In one of our great Tabernacle meetings, we had a special delegation. When we asked them to stand, and asked them what song they liked best, instead of calling out a number, they started to sing the song. They got it pitched too high, and when they came to the high place in the song, the voices broke, and in confusion they sat down with the great crowd laughing at them. They were very much embarrassed and disappointed. I told them the story of the old lady who always pitched the tunes in her church. This particular time the song was "He's the fairest of ten thousand to my soul." The high place in the song comes exactly on the "ten thousand." The old lady got it too high, and when she got to the high place, her voice broke. She tried it again, and again. After the third failure, a man in the back part of the church called out, "Sister, I believe I'd try it at five thousand once." This story turned the laughing of the people from the mistake of the crowd to the story. This also gave the pianist a chance to find the right pitch. I asked the crowd to stand again. We gave them a good, full chord. They started their song in the right key, sang it successfully, and everybody was happy.

It is also a splendid thing to slip an appropriate poem into your song service occasionally. For instance, you can ask them to sing in this way.

> "If you'll sing a song as you go along,
> In the face of a real or a fancied wrong,
> In spite of the doubt, if you'll fight it out,
> And show a heart that is brave and stout;
> If you'll laugh at the jeers, and refuse the tears,
> You'll force the ever reluctant cheers,
> That the world denies when a coward cries,
> And gives to the man who bravely tries,
> And you'll win success with a little song,
> If you'll sing the song as you go along."

Every good director should have a few songs among the most familiar ones which he can easily start even without a chord from the piano. Many times an emergency will arise when a song, started promptly and quickly, might even avert a panic, or at least an embarrassing situation.

One other kind of a song service that is always interesting and effective is to let the old folks select some of their favorite old hymns. Start them, if possible, without a piano, and sing them unaccompanied. This will bring some very happy and helpful memories to a lot of people.

With these suggestions and with this handbook, we are hoping to help you make all your song services more interesting and helpful to folks everywhere.

"The songs you sing
    And the smiles you wear
  Make the sunshine
      Everywhere."

Let us have more music "of the people, by the people, and for the people."

"If you'll sing a song as you trudge along,
  You'll find that the singing will make you strong,
  And the heavy load, and the rugged road,
  And the sting and the strife of the torturous goad
  Will soar with the note that you set afloat,
  That the beam will change to a trifling mote,
  That the world is bad when you are sad,
  And bright and beautiful when you are glad;
  And that all you need is a little song,
  If you'll sing the song as you trudge along."

1. Oh! Worship the King

TUNE: "*Lyons*"

ROBERT GRANT

J. MICHAEL HAYDN

A Scotchman, William Kethe, fled with the Protestant exiles from England to Frankfurt in 1555, and continued with them to Geneva in 1557, when they became embroiled in that famous theological controversy known then as "the troubles begonne at Franckford." At Geneva they found peace and Calvin and psalm-singing. In their effort to imitate in English the fine French metrical versions of the psalms that Calvin's congregations were using, William Kethe had an active part, composing twenty-five psalm versions for the Anglo-Genevan Psalter of 1561. One of these was "All people that on earth do dwell," a translation of Psalm 100 that is still in common use. It was written for Louis Bourgeois' tune, "Old Hundredth." Another was his translation of Psalm 104, "My soul, praise the Lord," which was brought back to England by the exiles when they returned, and passed into the Scottish Psalter of 1564 and the English Psalter of 1562.

Sir Robert Grant, a Privy Councillor in the British government, made a new version of William Kethe's metrical psalm, which was published in 1833 in Bickersteth's *Church Psalmody,* beginning with the line, "Oh! worship the King." He kept Kethe's original metre, but modernized the phraseology. The next year Sir Robert was made Governor of Bombay and, four years later, July 9, 1838, died in Dapoorie, West India.

TUNE: "Lyons" was composed by Johann Michael Haydn, the younger brother of the more famous, Franz Joseph Haydn. Born in Rohrau, Lower Austria, September 14, 1737, he became a famous composer and a skilled player of the violin and organ. He wrote much church music and played in various churches and the cathedral at Salzburg, in which city he died, August 10, 1806.

1

2. The Harp at Nature's Advent Strung

TUNE: *"Evan"*

John G. Whittier   William H. Havergal

The Quaker poet, Whittier, who wrote so many beautiful hymns, expressing his simple faith and trust in God, began his career humbly. Born in Haverhill, Massachusetts, December 17, 1807, he worked on a farm as a boy and then became a shoemaker, later developing his poetic ability. In 1845 he published a poem, "The Worship of Nature," describing nature's praise of God and containing lines, from which the hymn, "The green earth sends its incense up," was taken. Later, 1867, another hymn was selected as a cento from the same poem, "The harp at nature's advent strung," and was published in *The Tent on the Beach.* One editor, Dr. Charles L. Noyes, has discovered that these lines were possibly written by Whittier in his teens and were first published in the *Haverhill Gazette,* October 5, 1827. This earlier poem, revised, was woven into the longer poem, "The Worship of Nature," from which our present hymn was derived. He died in 1892.

TUNE: The Rev. William Henry Havergal (1793-1870) composed many anthems, psalm and hymn tunes, as well as songs and rounds. Those appearing in the periodical, *Our Own Fireside,* were later published as *Fireside Music.* His daughter, the famous hymn writer, Frances Ridley Havergal, edited his works after his death. The tune, "Evan," is one of the best of his melodies.

3. For the Beauty of the Earth

TUNE: *"Dix"*

Folliott S. Pierpoint   Conrad Kocher

A young man in his twenties, Folliott S. Pierpoint, seven years before he graduated from Queen's College, Cambridge University, with classical honors, wrote the joyous hymn of thanks to God, "For the beauty of the earth," to be sung at the Holy Communion services of the church. It first appeared in Orby Shipley's *Lyra Eucharistica,* second edition, 1864, with eight stanzas. In abridged form it is now used as a children's hymn, or for a congregational worship song.

2

TUNE: Conrad Kocher, composer of the tune, "Dix," was born in Stüttgart, 1786, taught music in Russia, studied *a capella* music in Italy, and in 1827 became director in the Stiftskirche, Stüttgart. He composed two operas, an oratorio and much church music. He died in 1872. (See No. 58.)

4. Angel Voices, Ever Singing

TUNE: *"Angel Voices"*

FRANCIS POTT

ARTHUR S. SULLIVAN

In 1861 the congregation of Wingates Church, Lancashire, England, were about to dedicate a new organ in their church and, wishing to signalize the event with a new hymn, they asked the Rev. Francis Pott, curate of Ardingly, Berkshire, to compose lines appropriate to the occasion. A few years out of Oxford (B.A. 1854, M.A. 1857), he was already becoming known for his fine hymn translations from the Latin and Syriac, and for some of his original hymns in English. The resulting lines he produced were most happy, "Angel voices, ever singing." It was, five years later, published in his *Hymns fitted to the Order of Common Prayer,* and originally was entitled, "For the Dedication of an Organ, or for a Meeting of Choirs." The author that year became rector of Norhill, Ely.

TUNE: The tune, "Angel Voices," which takes its title from the first two words of the Rev. Francis Pott's hymn, "Angel voices, ever singing," was composed by Sir Arthur S. Sullivan in 1871. (See No. 73.)

5. Praise the Lord, Ye Heavens, Adore Him

TUNE: *"Hymn to Joy"*

EDWARD OSLER

LUDWIG VAN BEETHOVEN

The original authorship of this hymn is in doubt. It first appears in a four-page folder, pasted in the back of *Psalms, Hymns, and Anthems of the Foundling Hospital,* of London. Dr. Edward Osler (born in Falmouth, January, 1798), who studied to be a physician with Doctor Carvasso at Falmouth and later at Guy's Hospital, London, was house surgeon at Swansea Infirmary, when he decided to give up medical practice and devote his energies to literature. He later became editor of the *Royal Cornwall Gazette,* wrote a few books, and composed many hymns. Impressed by the hymn, "Praise the Lord," which he may have seen in the Foundling Hospital book, he adapted it and added to it the whole of the third stanza, as it is now sung, beginning, "Worship, honor, glory, blessing." He died at Truro, March 7, 1863.

TUNE: From the final movement in Beethoven's Ninth Symphony was taken the melody, "Hymn to Joy." This is known as the Choral Symphony; for, after the former movements and a part of the last have been rendered, a singer suddenly interrupts the flow of purely instrumental music by challenging the other singers to lift their voices in praise and thanksgiving to God, and then chorus and orchestra blend in the thrilling "Hymn to Joy," based on Schiller's poem. (See No. 37.)

6. O God, the Rock of Ages

TUNE: *"Greenland"*

EDWARD H. BICKERSTETH   LAUSANNE PSALTER

"O God, the Rock of Ages" was written in 1860 or 1862 by a bishop of the Church of England, Dr. Edward H. Bickersteth (1825-1906), but a quarter of a century before his elevation to the episcopacy, the year (1885) when he was successively appointed Dean of Gloucester and Bishop of Exeter. It was a metrical version of some of the verses of Psalm 90; and, like so many of the psalmists' songs, it follows the three-part form, 1. Thesis, 2. Antithesis, 3. Synthesis. The Thesis, Part 1, usually contemplates the eternal greatness of God; the Antithesis, Part 2, pictures the weakness of man and the brevity of his life; the Synthesis, Part 3, brings man's weakness up to God's everlasting mercy and crowns him with eternal life. In this instance Part 1 consists of the first stanza, Part 2 of the second, and Part 3 of the third and fourth. (Compare No. 220, etc.)

TUNE: The tune, "Greenland," was taken from the Lausanne Psalter. Its composer is not known.

4

7. O Thou God of My Salvation

TUNE: *"Regent Square"*

THOMAS OLIVERS

HENRY SMART

Thomas Olivers, born at Tregynon, Montgomeryshire, England, in 1725, was left an orphan when he was a little over four years old. The relatives who brought him up, taking turns at the disagreeable task, neglected his mental and moral education. As a lad he was apprenticed to a cobbler; but his increasing wickedness became such a menace that at the age of eighteen he was driven out of town. After wandering through Shrewsbury and Wrexham, he came to Bristol, where he heard the eloquent George Whitefield preach a searching sermon on the text, "Is not this a brand plucked out of the fire?" He applied its lessons to himself, was then and there converted, and soon afterward joined the Methodist Society at Bradford-on-Avon. Here, just as he was starting up his trade as a cobbler, Wesley met him and set him to preaching in Cornwall in 1753. Later he helped edit the *Arminian Magazine,* and wrote both hymn-tunes and hymns. "O Thou God of my salvation" and "The God of Abraham praise" were his best. He died in London, March, 1799, and was buried in Wesley's tomb near City Road Chapel.

TUNE: Henry Smart (1813-1879) was a distinguished London organist who, though blind, won fame as a brilliant player and as composer of operas, cantatas, organ pieces, anthems and a number of our best hymn-tunes of the English cathedral type. "Regent Square" derives its title from a prominent square in London, on which stood St. Philip's Church where Smart was organist. It was first published in *Psalms and Tunes for Divine Worship,* 1867.

8. O for a Thousand Tongues to Sing

TUNE: *"Azmon"*

CHARLES WESLEY

CARL G. GLASER
Arranged by LOWELL MASON

"Glory to God, and praise and love" was the first line of an eighteen-stanza hymn, written by Charles Wesley in 1739, on the first anniversary of his conversion on Sunday,

May 21, 1738, and was entitled, "For the Anniversary Day of One's Conversion." R. Conyers in 1767 made a cento from this longer hymn, beginning with "O for a thousand tongues to sing," and consisting of stanzas 7 and 9-12, inclusive. This was published in his *Psalms and Hymns*. The first line of this cento is reminiscent of a remark made to Wesley by his Moravian friend, Peter Böhler: "Had I a thousand tongues, I would praise Him with them all." (See No. 100.)

TUNE: The melody of the hymn tune, "Azmon," was taken from the music of Carl G. Glaser, which he wrote in 1828. Glaser was born in Wessenfels, Germany, on May 4, 1784. He studied music under his father at home and afterwards in St. Thomas School, Leipzig, under Johann A. Hiller, August E. Muller and Campagnoli. Giving up the study of law which he had begun at Leipzig, he devoted his life to composing and to teaching the piano, vocal culture and the violin. He died at Barman, April 16, 1829. The present arrangement of the tune was made by Lowell Mason. (See No. 21.)

9. Come, Thou Almighty King

TUNE: *"Italian Hymn"*

ANONYMOUS   FELICE DE' GIARDINI

Although attributed to Charles Wesley, the authorship of "Come, Thou Almighty King" is unknown. Its earliest known printing was in a four-page tract where it appeared with six stanzas of Wesley's "Jesus, let Thy pitying eye"; but there is no evidence that Wesley wrote it. Entitled, "An Hymn to the Trinity," its form is adapted to the subject: the first stanza being addressed to the Almighty King, Father all-glorious; the second to Christ, the Incarnate Word; the third to the Holy Comforter; and the fourth to the Triune God, "great One in Three."

TUNE: The melody is called "Italian Hymn," not because it was composed in Italy, but because its composer, Felice de' Giardini (1716-1796), was an Italian violinist, conductor and composer of some distinction. He composed the tune while on concert tour in Russia.

10. We Praise Thee, O God, Our Redeemer, Creator

Tune: "*Kremser*"

Julia Bulkley Cady   Old Dutch Melody

Mrs. Robert H. Cory of Englewood, New Jersey, was before her marriage Miss Julia Bulkley Cady, the daughter of Cleveland Cady. In 1904 Archer Gibson, organist of the Brick Presbyterian Church, New York city, was preparing music for the Thanksgiving Day service in his church, and wished to use the old Dutch melody, known as "Kremser" in some of our hymnals. But the words, usually sung to that tune, he felt, were too militaristic and too vindictive in some of their expressions for use in a Christian service. Accordingly he asked her to write a new hymn for the tune, and to meet this need she penned her stirring hymn, "We praise Thee, O God, our Redeemer, Creator." It was first publicly rendered at the Brick Church service, the next Thanksgiving Day, and was first given hymnal publication in *Hymns of the Living Church,* 1910.

TUNE: This old Netherlands folk song was named "Kremser" because of the especially fine setting of it which was made by Edward Kremser (1838-1914), leader for thirty years of the Vienna Männergesangverein. He also arranged many other Netherlands songs.

11. Round the Lord in Glory Seated

Tune: "*Faben*"

Richard Mant   John H. Wilcox

Bishop Richard Mant, born in Southampton, England, in 1776, is hymnologically best known for his translations from the Latin, especially from the existing *Roman Breviary.* He also made a metrical translation of all the psalms. One of his finest original hymns is "Bright the vision that delighted," published in 1837, and entitled, "Hymn Commemorative of the 'Thrice Holy.'" From this was taken the cento, "Round the Lord in glory

7

seated." The author began his ministry as curate to his father. After serving as vicar of Coggeshill, he became chaplain to the Archbishop of Canterbury, rector of St. Botolph, London, and of East Horsley. Then he became Bishop of Killaloe, 1820, of Down and Connor, 1823, and of Dromore, 1842, until his death, November 2, 1848.

TUNE: The tune, "Faben," was composed by Dr. John Henry Wilcox, an American composer, who was born in 1827, won the degree of Doctor of Music through his compositions in church music, and died in 1875.

12. We Lift Our Hearts to Thee

TUNE: *"Mornington"*

JOHN WESLEY

EARL OF MORNINGTON

John Wesley's hymn, "We lift our hearts to Thee," was first found in his *A Collection of Psalms and Hymns,* 1741, under the title, "A Morning Hymn," and is one of the few Wesleyan hymns known to have been written by John Wesley, rather than by his brother, Charles (who wrote over six thousand original hymns). John Wesley, however, translated a number of hymns from the German and some from the French. Though this hymn was originally an English hymn, one of its phrases is a rendering of the Latin sentence from Plato, "Lumen est umbra Dei"; it is the third line of the first stanza, "The sun itself is but Thy shade." The Rev. John Wesley, born at Epworth, England, 1703, was made a Fellow of Lincoln College, Oxford, 1729, after his graduation. Returning from a missionary journey to Georgia, U. S. A., he became conscious of sins forgiven on May 24, 1738, and started the Wesleyan revival whereby he became the Founder of Methodism. He died in 1791.

TUNE: Garrett Colley Wellesley (1735-1781), who was the Earl of Mornington, was educated at Dublin University, where he was later professor, 1764-1774. He composed many glees, madrigals and church tunes. He was the father of the famous Duke of Wellington. From his well-known "Chant in E" a hymn-tune arrangement was made in short meter and thus the tune, "Mornington," was published in Miller's *David's Harp,* 1805.

13. Awake, My Soul, and with the Sun

TUNE: *"Morning Hymn"*

THOMAS KEN   FRANCOIS H. BARTHELEMON

Julian's *Dictionary of Hymnology* states that this hymn is one of the four which stand at the head of all hymns in the English language; the other three being "Hark! the herald angels sing," "Rock of Ages, cleft for me," and "When I survey the wondrous cross." "Awake, my soul" was written as a Morning Hymn for the boys of Winchester College, and published in the 1695 edition of *A Manual of Prayers for the Use of the Scholars of Winchester College,* and with some variations in the 1709 edition. Like Ken's Evening Hymn, "Glory to Thee, my God, this night," and his Midnight Hymn, "Lord, now my sleep does me forsake," written for the same purpose and published at the same time, it ends with Ken's famous doxology, "Praise God from whom all blessings flow." The quaint 1695 version contained this third line of the doxology, "Praise Him above y' Angelick Host." · Bishop Thomas Ken (1637-1711), an Oxford graduate, was made Bishop of Bath and Wells by King Charles II. But later refusing to publish the "Declaration of Indulgence," he was imprisoned in the Tower of London by the Catholic King James II. After his release, his later years he spent in retirement.

TUNE: A French composer, who was born in Bordeaux, France, 1741, and died in London, 1808, François Hippolyte Barthélemon, started his career as an army officer in an Irish brigade. Later he became a professional musician, toured Europe as a violinist, and composed operas and theatre music and also an oratorio. The Rev. Jacob Duché, chaplain of the Female Orphan Asylum, led him to compose this tune to Bishop Ken's Morning Hymn.

14. When Morning Gilds the Skies

TUNE: *"Laudes Domini"*

Translated from the German by EDWARD CASWALL   JOSEPH BARNBY

"Beim frühen Morgenlicht," a German hymn of the early nineteenth century, was sometimes called "The Christian Greeting." No one knows who wrote it, though it is supposed to be Franconian in its origin. From one of the several German versions in which it appeared, the Rev. Edward Caswall (1814-1878), a famous translator especially of Latin hymns, made the translation, "When morning gilds the skies," and it was first published in H. Formby's *Catholic Hymns,* 1854, and later in Caswall's *Masque of Mary,* 1858, when eight new stanzas were added to the original six. In 1847 Caswall resigned as a clergyman of the Church of England at Stratford-sub-Castle, and three years later followed Dr. John Henry Newman into the Roman Catholic Church.

TUNE: The tune, "Laudes Domini," was first printed in the Appendix to *Hymns Ancient and Modern,* 1868, and later in Barnby's *Hymns with Tunes,* 1869. Its Latin title means "Praise to the Master," derived from this hymn. Its composer, Sir Joseph Barnby (1838-1896), wrote 246 hymn-tunes and edited five hymn-books, the most famous being *The Hymnary.* He gained distinction in England as an organist, choral conductor and composer of the oratorio, "Rebekah," and a large mass of church music.

15. Still, Still with Thee

TUNE: *"Willingham"*

HARRIET BEECHER STOWE   FRANZ ABT

Mrs. Harriet Beecher Stowe was in the midst of the immense excitement over her anti-slavery novel, *Uncle Tom's Cabin,* which first appeared in *The National Era* in 1852, when her brother, Dr. Henry Ward Beecher, produced his famous hymn-book, *Plymouth Collection.* This book contained "Still, still with Thee when purple morning breaketh," and two other hymns by Mrs. Stowe. (See No. 178.)

TUNE: The son of a clergyman, Franz Abt (1819-1885), studied both music and theology at the University of Leipzig, but finally devoted his life-work to music, composing over four hundred works, chiefly songs, from one of which the hymn-tune, "Willingham," has been adapted to Mrs. Stowe's morning hymn.

16.   O Father, Hear My Morning Prayer

TUNE: *"Eversley"*

MRS. F. A. PERCY   ARTHUR COTTMAN

Mrs. Frances A. Percy's hymn, "O Father, hear my morning prayer," first appeared in *Hymns of Faith and Life,* 1896, edited by Dr. John Hunter.

TUNE: Arthur Cottman was an English lawyer who was interested in music. He was born in 1842 and died in 1879. Among his compositions is the hymn-tune, "Eversley."

17.   Come, My Soul, Thou Must be Waking

TUNE: *"Haydn"*

F. R. L. VON CANITZ
Translated by H. J. BUCKOLL   From FRANZ JOSEPH HAYDN

The German hymn, "Seele du musst munter werden," by Baron Friedrich Rudolph Ludwig von Canitz (1654-1699), distinguished privy counsellor and dignitary at the court of Emperor Leopold I, was said to be a mirror of his life. H. J. Buckoll's translation, which has become our hymn, "Come, my soul, thou must be waking," was appended to the following note to a passage in Sermon 6 on Col. 3, 3, in Dr. Arnold's *Christian Life: Its Cause, Its Hindrances, and Its Helps,* London, 1841:

Some may know the story of that German nobleman (von Canitz) whose life had been distinguished alike by genius and worldly distinctions, and by Christian holiness; and who, in the last morning of his life, when the dawn broke into his sick-chamber, prayed that he might be supported to the window, and might look once again upon the rising sun. After looking steadily at it for some time, he cried out, "Oh! if the appearance of this earthly and created thing is so beautiful and quickening, how much more shall I be enraptured at the sight of the unspeakable glory of the Creator Himself."

TUNE: Francis Joseph Haydn (1732-1809), famous Austrian composer, is best known for his symphonies (he wrote 125), chamber works, and his oratorios, especially "Creation." (See No. 42.) This hymn-tune, taken from one of his works, bears his name, "Haydn."

11

18. Every Morning Mercies New

TUNE: *"Every Morning"*

GREVILLE PHILLIMORE   EDWARD J. HOPKINS

"Every morning they are new" is the way the Rev. Greville Phillimore (1821-1881), then a vicar and later a rector in the Church of England, originally wrote the first line of his morning hymn for the *Parish Hymn Book,* of which he and Bishop J. R. Woodford and H. W. Beadon were editors. It was altered to our present form when published in the *Hymnary,* 1872.

TUNE: The famous English organist, Dr. Edward J. Hopkins (1818-1901), composed twenty-five anthems and much other church music, including some of our best known hymn-tunes. He also wrote an authoritative book on *The Organ, Its History and Construction,* and edited the music of *The Temple Church Choral Service.* He was organist of the Temple Church, London, for fifty-five years.

19. New Every Morning Is the Love

TUNE: *"Canonbury"*

JOHN KEBLE   ROBERT SCHUMANN

John Keble's *Christian Year,* a book of sacred poems, published in 1827, is one of the classics in English literature. It opens with a poem of sixteen stanzas, "Hues of the rich unfolding morn," from which the popular hymn, "New every morning is the love" (sixth stanza), was taken. (See No. 25.)

TUNE: The tune, "Canonbury," is the melody of a piano piece, "Nachtstück" (Night Piece), Opus 23, No. 4, by Robert Schumann (1810-1856), the celebrated German composer. Schumann's great songs and larger works for orchestra and piano have won for him a great place in musical history.

20. O Day of Rest and Gladness

TUNE: *"Mendebras"*

CHRISTOPHER WORDSWORTH   Arranged by LOWELL MASON

Bishop Christopher Wordsworth in 1869 became Bishop of Lincoln in England, an office which he held for fifteen years until shortly before his death, March 20, 1885. He sought in his hymns chiefly to teach sound doctrine, whether the theme lent itself to poetry or not. The result was that few of his hymns were so truly poetical as the hymn on the Sabbath Day, "O day of rest and gladness."

TUNE: The hymn-tune, "Mendebras," was taken by Lowell Mason (see No. 21) from the melody of a German student song. Mason made some modifications in the tune, one of which was in ending on the tonic, where the original tune ended on the third note of the scale.

21. Safely Through Another Week

TUNE: *"Sabbath Morn"*

JOHN NEWTON   LOWELL MASON

The Rev. John Newton originally wrote his hymn, "Safely through another week," under the title, "Saturday Evening," and as such it first appeared in Newton's and Cowper's *Olney Hymns, 1779.* But in order to adapt it as a Sabbath hymn, a number of lines have been altered, and now it is often heard in Sabbath morning worship. (See No. 66.)

TUNE: Lowell Mason (1792-1872), composer of "Sabbath Morn," was a life-long exponent of better church music in America. To that end he widely organized and conducted singing classes and edited many collections of songs and hymns. His original hymn-tunes were many, among the most popular being this "Sabbath Morn," taking its title from the thought of John Newton's words.

22. Light of the World, We Hail Thee

TUNE: *"Salve Domine"*

JOHN S. B. MONSELL   LAWRENCE W. WATSON

The author of the hymn, "Light of the world, we hail Thee," the Rev. John S. B. Monsell, LL.D., was the son of Archdeacon Thomas B. Monsell of Londonderry. He became chaplain to Bishop Mant, chancellor of the diocese of Connor, rector of Ramoan, vicar of Egham, and rector of St. Nicholas's, Guilford. While they were rebuilding his church, on April 9, 1875, he fell from the roof and was killed. "Light of the world, we hail Thee," a missionary hymn, first appeared in his *Hymns of Love and Praise,* 1863.

TUNE: Lawrence White Watson, born in 1860, wrote his tune, "Salve Domine," in 1909. It is singularly well-adapted to Doctor Monsell's hymn.

23. Christ, Whose Glory Fills the Skies

TUNE: *"Lux Prima"*

CHARLES WESLEY   CHARLES F. GOUNOD

It was James Montgomery who in his *Christian Psalmist,* 1825, restored the name of Charles Wesley to the authorship of this hymn, after these lines, "Christ whose glory fills the skies," had been mistakenly attributed to A. M. Toplady for half a century. Montgomery called this hymn "one of C. Wesley's loveliest progeny." Sometimes the first line is given thus, "Thou, whose glory fills the skies." It has found wide use in this country. R. Bingham made an excellent Latin translation of it in 1871, beginning, "Christe, cujus gloriae." (See No. 100.)

TUNE: "Lux Prima" (whose Latin title means "First Light," or "Dawn," evidently derived from the thought of Wesley's hymn) was taken from a melody occurring in the works of Charles F. Gounod and rearranged as a hymn-tune. Gounod (1818-1893) was a great French composer of operas ("Faust," 1859, "Romeo and Juliet," 1867, etc.) and of oratorios ("Redemption," 1882, "Mors et Vita," 1885) and of many cantatas, masses, songs and instrumental works. His quickened religious interest induced him to abandon opera composing, and after 1881 he wrote almost exclusively sacred music.

24. Lord, on Thy Returning Day

TUNE: *"Holy Day"*

THOMAS T. LYNCH   JOHN H. GOWER

The Rivulet: a Contribution to Sacred Song in its first edition, published in London by Longman in 1855, contained the first publication of a number of the Rev.

14

Thomas T. Lynch's hymns, including "Lord, on Thy returning day." This book started a long and bitter controversy in the Congregational Church of England, which today is hard to understand, because time and a juster judgment have brought favor and widespread popularity to many of his hymns. Lynch entered the ministry as pastor of a small church at Highgate in 1847, later serving churches on Mortimer Street and Grafton Street, Fitzroy Square. From 1856 to 1859 he was incapacitated by illness; but from 1860 until his death on May 9, 1871, he served his old congregation on Gower Street and in their new place of worship (1862) in Hampstead Road. Julian says: "Lynch's hymns are marked by intense individuality, gracefulness and felicity of diction, picturesqueness, spiritual freshness, and the sadness of a powerful soul struggling with a weak and emaciated body."

TUNE: John Henry Gower, born in England in 1855, came to this country as a young man and won distinction as an organist, notably in the Cathedral in Denver, Colorado. His hymn-tune, "Holy Day," one of many of his which have been published, was composed in 1895, though he afterward altered it from its original form. Since his death, his tunes have been increasing in popularity.

25. Sun of My Soul
TUNE: *"Hursley"*

JOHN KEBLE

PETER RITTER
Arranged by WILLIAM H. MONK

The Rev. John Keble was in 1831 elected to the Poetry Professorship at Oxford University, and while still in that chair, two years later, 1833, he preached his famous Assize Sermon at Oxford which Dr. John H. Newman regarded as the start of the Oxford Movement, the revival of ancient authority and traditions in the Church of England. The Oxford Movement produced many fine hymns, and among them, "Sun of my soul," which was taken (like others of Keble's hymns) from his long poem, *The Christian Year.* He died in 1866.

TUNE: The tune, "Hursley," was arranged by the London organist, William H. Monk, from an ancient melody used in Roman Catholic worship, and probably derived from the Gregorian. It was first associated with the Rev. John Keble's hymn, "Sun of my soul," in *Metrical Psalter* by Henry Lahee, 1855, and is named "Hursley" from the parish in which Keble served. (See No. 31.)

26. Softly the Silent Night

TUNE: *"Blatchford"*

AMBROSE N. BLATCHFORD   ANONYMOUS

The Rev. Ambrose N. Blatchford, born in Plymouth, England, 1842, was graduated from London University, and became a Unitarian clergyman. His hymn, "Softly the silent night," like a number of other hymns from his pen, was written for one of the Sunday school anniversaries at Lewin's Mead Meeting (in this instance for the anniversary of 1875). It was first published in the *Sunday School Hymn Book* of the Sunday School Association in London, 1881.

TUNE: Neither the composer nor the origin of the tune, "Blatchford," is known. It was obviously named for the author of this hymn, "Softly the silent night."

27. God, That Madest Earth and Heaven

TUNE: *"Ar Hyd Nos"*

REGINALD HEBER
RICHARD WHATELY   WELSH MELODY

Long before Reginald Heber (1783-1826) was made Bishop of Calcutta (1823) for the Church of England, he felt the need of a higher literary quality in Christian hymns, and he sought eagerly among existing books of poetry for passages adaptable for hymns of real poetic value, stimulated some of his contemporary poets to write hymns, and himself composed a number of them of real literary merit, as well as spiritual power. His bishop would not permit him to publish this fine anthology of literary hymns that he had made; but after he himself had become a bishop and had died on the missionary field, at

Trinchinopoly, India, April 3, 1826, his widow published his collection posthumously, *Hymns Written and Adapted to the Weekly Church Service of the Year,* and this book has had an immeasurable influence, introducing into Christion worship such hymns as "God, that madest earth and heaven," "Holy, holy, holy, Lord God almighty," "The Son of God goes forth to war," and "Brightest and best of the sons of the morning."

TUNE: "Ar Hyd Nos" is a popular traditional Welsh melody, to which the song, "All through the night," is frequently sung.

28. Now the Day Is Over

TUNE: *"Merrial"*

SABINE BARING-GOULD

JOSEPH BARNBY

When the Rev. Sabine Baring-Gould was thirty-one years old, one year after his ordination as minister of the Church of England, he was serving as curate at Horbury, near Wakefield, 1865. He felt the need of some special hymns for the little group of poor people to whom he ministered in the Sabbath services in a second-story room; and it was for them he penned the simple and beautiful hymn, "Now the day is over." It was printed that year in *Church Times* and three years later in the Appendix to *Hymns Ancient and Modern.*

TUNE: The tune, "Merrial," was composed by Sir Joseph Barnby. (See No. 14.)

29. Softly Now the Light of Day

TUNE: *"Seymour"*

GEORGE WASHINGTON DOANE

Arranged from
CARL MARIA VON WEBER

Bishop Doane, named for George Washington because he was born in the year when the Father of his Country died, 1799, became at the age of twenty-five a professor in Trinity College, Hartford, Connecticut, and four years later, rector of Trinity Church, Boston. In 1837, five years after he became Bishop of New Jersey, he founded

St. Mary's Hall, in Burlington, New Jersey, a church school for girls. He called the institution "the jewel of the diocese." It was in one of the ground-floor rooms of this school, its windows overlooking a scene of rare beauty, at a bend in the Delaware River, that the good bishop at the twilight hour wrote "Softly now the light of day."

TUNE: Baron Carl Maria von Weber (1786-1826) was one of Germany's great composers of operas, symphonies, songs and piano sonatas. From his opera, "Oberon," 1826, was taken the hymn-tune, "Seymour."

30. Day Is Dying in the West

TUNE: *"Evening Praise"*

MARY A. LATHBURY   WILLIAM F. SHERWIN

Miss Lathbury was *par excellence* the poet of Chautauqua. In the summer of 1880, Dr. John H. Vincent (afterwards bishop) requested her to write a Vesper Song for the evening services of the summer conference at Chautauqua, New York, and also for the Chautauqua Circles throughout the country. She eagerly responded with this evening hymn of worship and praise, "Day is dying in the west." (See No. 120.)

TUNE: The tune, "Evening Praise," was composed by William Fisk Sherwin (1826-1887) especially for Miss Lathbury's hymn, "Day is dying in the west." He wrote a large number of hymn-tunes for Sunday school and church worship, and many of these he popularized at Chautauqua. (See No. 120.)

31. Abide with Me! Fast Falls the Eventide

TUNE: *"Eventide"*

HENRY F. LYTE   WILLIAM H. MONK

The story of the writing of "Abide with me" by the Rev. Henry F. Lyte shortly before he died is told by his daughter, Anna Maria Maxwell Hogg, in a preface to his *Remains:*

The summer was passing away, and the month of September (that month in which he was once more to quit his native land), arrived, and each day seemed to have a special value as being one

18

day nearer his departure. His family were surprised and almost alarmed at his announcing his intention of preaching once more to his people. His weakness, and the possible danger attending the effort, were urged to prevent it, but in vain. "It was better," as he used often playfully to say, when in comparative health, "to *wear* out than to rust out." He felt that he should be enabled to fulfil his wish, and feared not for the result. His expectation was well founded. He did preach, and amid the breathless attention of his hearers gave them the sermon on the Holy Communion, which is inserted last in this volume (i. e. *Remains*). He afterwards assisted at the administration of the Holy Eucharist, and though necessarily much exhausted by the exertion and excitement of this effort, yet his friends had no reason to believe it had been hurtful to him. In the evening of the same day he placed in the hands of a near and dear relative the little hymn, "Abide with me," with an air of his own composing, adapted to the words. (See No. 208.)

TUNE: The tune, "Eventide," was composed by William H. Monk. Mrs. Monk once wrote this account of its composition in a letter to Mr. J. C. Hadden:

This tune was written at a time of great sorrow—when together we watched, as we did daily, the glories of the setting sun. As the last golden ray faded, he took up some paper and pencilled that tune, which has gone over all the earth. (See No. 233.)

32. All Praise to Thee, My God, This Night

TUNE: *"Tallis's Canon"*

THOMAS KEN   THOMAS TALLIS

"Glory to Thee, my God, this night" is another version of the first line of the Evening Hymn by Bishop Thomas Ken. The lines were written for the students of Bishop Ken's old Alma Mater, Winchester College, as was also his Morning Hymn. (See No. 13.)

TUNE: "Tallis's Canon" is one of the most interesting hymn-tunes, both from its antiquity and its form. Stainer and Barrett's *Dictionary* says: "The essence of a canon is this, that the music of one part shall, after a short rest, be sung by another part, note for note." In this instance, after the soprano has sung the first four notes (to "All praise to Thee"), the tenor then repeats the same four notes (to "my God, this night") and continues throughout the tune, just one measure behind the soprano, completing the melody on the first four words of the next stanza.

It first appeared in *The Whole Psalter*, 1560, published anonymously, but evidently by Matthew Parker, Archbishop of Canterbury, whose name in Latin, Mattheus Parkerus, appears in acrostic in the introduction to Psalm 119. The melody is one of nine by Tallis at the end of the book, being set to Psalm 67. Bishop Ken, himself, probably adapted the tune to his own hymn.

Thomas Tallis or Tallys (1520-1585) was organist in Queen Elizabeth's Royal Chapel, has been called "the father of English Cathedral music," and composed much important church music, which bridged over the traditions of Roman Catholic worship in the development of the post-Reformation era.

33. Saviour, Again to Thy Dear Name
TUNE: *"Ellers"*

JOHN ELLERTON   EDWARD J. HOPKINS

This has become the most successful of fifty hymns, written by the Rev. John Ellerton, a clergyman of the Church of England, who was born in London, 1826. It was written in five four-line stanzas for the 1866 festival of the Malpas, Middlewich, and Nantwich Choral Association. Ellerton served many churches as vicar and rector, and was one year Canon of St. Albans, until his death in 1893. With Bishop How he edited *Church Hymns,* 1871, and was author of *Notes and Illustrations of Church Hymns,* 1881.

TUNE: The tune, "Ellers," by Dr. Edward J. Hopkins (see No. 18) was first published in Brown-Borthwick's *Supplemental Tune-Book,* 1869. It was written for unison singing and so appeared at first; but later it was harmonized for four voices and in this form was included in the appendix to the *Bradford Tune-Book.*

34. The Shadows of the Evening Hours
TUNE: *"St. Leonard"*

ADELAIDE A. PROCTER   HENRY HILES

Miss Adelaide Anne Procter, the daughter of Bryan Waller Procter (Barry Cornwall), was born in London, 1825. A fine musician and linguist of much ability, she became known most widely as a poet. In her *Legends and Lyrics, a Book of Verse,* 1862, there first appeared this tenderly beautiful evening hymn, "The shadows of the evening hours," written eleven years after her admission into the Roman Church (1851), and two years before her death (1864).

TUNE: Henry Hiles (1826-1904), composer of the hymn-tune, "St. Leonard," was a distinguished English organist and musical theorist, became professor in the Royal College of Music, 1893, and conducted oratorio societies. His oratorios are well known, especially "The Crusaders," and his compositions have entered many different fields.

35. On Our Way Rejoicing

TUNE: *"Hermas"*

JOHN S. B. MONSELL

FRANCES R. HAVERGAL

"On our way rejoicing" was first written by the Rev. John S. B. Monsell of the Church of England, to be sung on the first Sunday after Trinity, and was first published in his book, *Hymns of Love and Praise*, 1863. Afterwards, he rewrote it for his *Parish Hymnal*, 1873, with the first four lines used as a refrain. This has made the hymn better adapted for processional uses. (See No. 22.)

TUNE: Miss Frances Ridley Havergal, known chiefly as a hymn writer, inherited much of her musical ability from her father, the Rev. W. H. Havergal, who was a composer; and she occasionally wrote tunes of her own. "Hermas" she composed for her own hymn, "Golden harps are sounding." (See No. 110.)

36. Lord, Dismiss Us with Thy Blessing

TUNE: *"Sicilian Mariners"*

JOHN FAWCETT

ITALIAN

Some hymnologists believe that this hymn (which is one of four beginning with the same first line) was written by the Rev. Walter Shirley; but the preponderance of evidence favors the Rev. Dr. John Fawcett as author, a Baptist Minister of the eighteenth century, living and preaching in Yorkshire, England. Sometimes the first line of this popular Dismissal Hymn is given, "Lord, *refresh* us with Thy blessing," and sometimes "Lord, *enrich* us with Thy blessing." (See No. 217.)

TUNE: The tune, "Sicilian Mariners," is a traditional Italian melody of unknown authorship, often sung to the Latin hymn, "O sanctissima, O purissima."

37. May the Grace of Christ

TUNE: *"Sardis"*

JOHN NEWTON   LUDWIG VAN BEETHOVEN

This benediction hymn, a paraphrase of 2 Cor. 13, 14, was penned by the Rev. John Newton when he was curate at Olney, and published in the *Olney Hymns,* in which Newton collaborated with the English poet, William Cowper. Bingham's Latin translation of this hymn begins with the line, "Gratia nostri Salvatoris." (See No. 66.)

TUNE: Ludwig van Beethoven (1770-1827), regarded by many as the greatest composer who ever lived, and by all as the founder of the new progress in composition in the nineteenth century, was born in Bonn, though his work was done chiefly in Vienna, where the Elector subsidized him. His fame rests chiefly on his nine symphonies.

38. There's a Wideness in God's Mercy

TUNE: *"Wellesley"*

FREDERICK W. FABER   LIZZIE S. TOURJEE

Originally a clergyman in the Church of England, Frederick W. Faber (1814-1863) seceded to the Church of Rome in 1846. He felt the lack among the Catholics of such hymns of popular appeal as the Wesleys had used and as the *Olney Hymns* had proved to be; and he set about supplying that need by writing hymns of simplicity and fervor, such as this hymn on the "wideness in God's mercy." At first he wrote twelve hymns for the schools at St. Wilfrid's and later expanded this number into 150, some of which have become very popular among Protestants, as well as Catholics.

TUNE: Miss Lizzie S. Tourjee, who on August 16, 1883, became Mrs. Franklin Estabrook, was about to graduate from Newton (Mass.) High School, when she was asked to compose a tune for the graduation hymn. The result was the tune, "Wellesley," named for a woman's college in a neighboring town. Her father, Dr. Eben Tourjee, director of the New England Conservatory of Music, Boston, when he became musical editor of *The Methodist Episcopal Hymnal*, 1878, included her tune, set here to Father Faber's "There's a wideness."

39. Holy, Holy, Holy, Lord God Almighty

TUNE: *"Nicæa"*

REGINALD HEBER

JOHN B. DYKES

Bishop Heber wrote his noble hymn of worship of the Trinity, as a metrical paraphrase of Revelation 4, 8-11; and it was designed to be used on Trinity Sunday. It was published after his death in the *Hymns Written and Adapted to the Weekly Church Service of the Year* (see note on No. 27), and has proved to be the most popular of all the hymns in that hymnal of rare literary excellence. In order to make it adaptable for any time of day, and not merely for early morning, the second line, "Early in the morning our song shall rise to Thee," has sometimes been changed to "Gratefully adoring, our song," or "Morning and evening, our song," or "Holy, holy, holy, our song," or "Morning, noon, and night, our song"; the first of these alterations being most preferred. (See No. 27.)

TUNE: The hymn being on the theme of the Trinity, the tune, especially written by Dr. Dykes for these words, is happily entitled, "Nicæa," after the city where the Nicæan Creed of the Trinity was adopted and promulgated. The tune appeared in *Hymns Ancient and Modern*, 1861. (See No. 113.)

40. Rejoice, Ye Pure in Heart

TUNE: *"Marion"*

EDWARD H. PLUMPTRE

ARTHUR H. MESSITER

The Rev. Dr. Edward Hayes Plumptre, distinguished theologian and preacher of the Church of England (born

in London, 1821), was asked to write a hymn for the
Peterborough Choral Festival in May, 1865, and in response to this request composed "Rejoice, ye pure in
heart," which was first sung in Peterborough Cathedral.
It is the best known of Plumptre's many hymns.

TUNE: Arthur Henry Messiter (1834-1916) from
1866 until 1897 was organist of Trinity Protestant Episcopal Church, New York city, at the west end of Wall
Street. In 1907 he wrote a history of the music of that
church, and in 1865 composed this tune, "Marion," for a
festival of the choir of Peterborough Cathedral in England,
his native land. He was born in Frome, Somersetshire.

41. Thou Rulest, Lord, the Lights on High

TUNE: *"De Pauw"*

THEODORE WILLIAMS   ROBERT G. McCUTCHAN

The Rev. Dr. Theodore Williams was a prominent
Unitarian clergyman, who for many years served as pastor
of All Souls' Church, New York city, and also as head-
master of Hackley School on Tarrytown, New York. He
wrote many hymns, which since his death are still being
widely sung; and one of the best of these is "Thou rulest,
Lord, the lights on high."

TUNE: Dean Robert G. McCutchan composed his
tune, "De Pauw," for Dr. Williams's hymn, "Thou rulest,
Lord," in 1928, especially for *Standard Hymns and Gospel
Songs,* and named it for De Pauw University in Green-
castle, Indiana, where he is Dean of the School of Music.
(See No. 105.)

42. The Spacious Firmament on High

TUNE: *"Creation"*

JOSEPH ADDISON   FRANCIS J. HAYDN

Joseph Addison's primacy as a finished writer of English
prose in the fore part of the eighteenth century came to
be recognized largely through his contributions to literary

periodicals, *The Spectator, Tatler, Guardian* and *The Freeholder.* In the first of these appeared a number of poems or hymns, used in essays from Addison's pen and attributed to his composition. The issue of August 23, 1712, contained the magnificent hymn on creation, based largely on Psalm 19, 1-6, "The spacious firmament on high."

TUNE: The melody of the hymn-tune, "Creation," is taken from the chorus, "The heavens are telling," in the oratorio, "Creation," by Francis Joseph Haydn. (See No. 17). It was completed in 1798. Haydn has said of this work: "Never was I so pious as when composing the 'Creation.' I knelt down every day and prayed God to strengthen me for my work."

43. Guide Me, O Thou Great Jehovah

TUNE: *"Zion"*

WILLIAM WILLIAMS

THOMAS HASTINGS

William Williams (1717-1791) of Pantycelyn came to be famed as "the Sweet Singer of Wales." At the age of twenty-three he was ordained a deacon in the Established Church, but never became a priest. For thirty-five years he preached in various parts of Wales, being especially effective in revival preaching. His first hymn-book, *Halleluiah,* was published in 1744 and his second, *Y Mor o Wydr,* in 1762. His most popular hymn is "Guide me, O Thou great Jehovah," which was translated from the Welsh by the Rev. Peter Williams in 1771, and in 1774 appeared in George Whitefield's *Collection* under the title, "Christ a Sure Guide."

TUNE: Thomas Hastings (1787-1872), a popular New York singing teacher, united his efforts with those of Lowell Mason to improve hymn-singing in America. He edited many hymn-books, wrote sixty hymns and a number of hymn-tunes. The tune, "Zion," was published in *Spiritual Songs for Social Worship,* 1831, by Lowell Mason and Thomas Hastings, here set to Thomas Kelly's "On the mountain's top appearing," with its frequent reference to Zion: hence its title, "Zion."

44.   Oh, Give Thanks to Him Who Made

Tune: *"Winona"*

Joseph Conder   Robert G. McCutchan

Joseph, or Josiah, Conder was the son of an engineer and bookseller, Thomas Conder, and he himself became well known as a publisher, author and editor. His chief periodical was the *Eclectic Review*. His poetical works and hymn-books were many. In his *The Congregational Hymn Book: a Supplement to Dr. Watts's Psalms and Hymns,* 1836, there first appeared his hymn on Thanksgiving for Daily Mercies, "O give thanks to Him who made."

TUNE: The tune, composed by Dean Robert G. McCutchan to this hymn and for this book, was named "Winona" for Winona Lake, Indiana, where he has appeared a number of times as lecturer and choral director in the Summer School of Religious Music. (See No. 105.)

45.   Let Us with a Gladsome Mind

Tune: *"Monkland"*

Psalm 136: John Milton   Arranged by John B. Wilkes

John Milton (1608-1674), the writer of the greatest epics in English poetry, composed nineteen known versions of psalms, many of them during the period of his blindness. His paraphrase of Psalm 136, however, was written when he was fifteen years old and was published in his *Poems in English and Latin,* 1645, "Let us with a gladsome mind."

TUNE: The tune, "Monkland," first published anonymously, 1824, in *Hymn Tunes of the United Brethren,* was republished in *Hymns Ancient and Modern,* 1861, with a new arrangement by Wilkes. He was organist in the church, of which the editor, Sir Henry W. Baker, was then vicar, at Monkland, and the tune was named for this place.

46. The Lord Jehovah Reigns

TUNE: *"Millennium"*

ISAAC WATTS

COMPOSER UNKNOWN

Isaac Watts, who overthrew the influence of the metrical psalms by writing "man-made" hymns in English that became acceptable for congregational worship, has been styled (somewhat loosely) "the Father of the English hymn." "The Lord Jehovah reigns," which has become one of his most widely used hymns, was published in *Hymns and Spiritual Songs,* 1709, but (strangely enough) it did not reappear in his *Psalms of David,* 1719. (See No. 174.)

TUNE: The composer and origin of the tune, "Millennium," are unknown.

47. A Mighty Fortress Is Our God

TUNE: *"Ein' Feste Burg"*

MARTIN LUTHER

MARTIN LUTHER

The German poet, Heine, spoke advisedly when he styled Luther's great hymn "the Marseillaise Hymn of the modern Reformation," but erred in stating that it was defiantly sung by Luther and his friends on their way to the Diet of Worms, 1521; for it was not composed until after that crucial event, and probably not until 1529. D'Aubigne wrote of it:

Luther, full of faith, revived the courage of his friends by composing and singing with his fine voice that beautiful hymn, since become so famous, "Ein' feste Burg ist unser Gott." Never did soul that knew its own weakness, but which, looking to God, despised every fear, find such noble accents. This hymn was sung during the Diet, not only at Augsburg, but in all the churches of Saxony, and its energetic strains often revived and inspirited the most dejected hearts.

TUNE: "Ein' Feste Burg," the strong chorale tune by Martin Luther, taking its title from the German first line of the hymn, to which it is sung, has proved a fit musical medium for the expression of such courageous sentiments. Some of the great composers have elaborated its theme in their larger compositions: Meyerbeer in "The

Huguenots," Mendelssohn in his "Reformation Symphony," fifth movement, and Wagner in his "Kaisermarsch."

48. Thou Art, O God, the Life and Light

TUNE: *"Pater Omnium"*

THOMAS MOORE   H. J. E. HOLMES

The Irish poet, Thomas Moore, was born in Dublin, May 28, 1779, the son of a small tradesman. Besides the many general poems found in his *Collected Works,* there was a group of *Sacred Songs,* 1816, some of which have passed into the hymnals, such as "Come, ye disconsolate," and this hymn, "Thou art, O God, the life and light." (See No. 202.)

TUNE: H. J. E. Holmes, an English composer, who wrote the tune, "Pater Omnium," was born in London in 1852. The tune takes its title from the Latin words for "Father of all."

49. Mighty God, While Angels Bless Thee

TUNE: *"Alleluia (Lowe)"*

ROBERT ROBINSON   ALBERT LOWE

Benjamin Williams in his advanced years told the story that when he was a small boy, the Rev. Robert Robinson (Baptist English clergyman, 1735-1790) visited his home and took him upon his knee to talk with him. Robinson's love for the child and desire for his salvation led him to write,

Mighty God, while angels bless Thee,
May an infant praise Thy name.

The second line has been altered for congregational use. Williams all the rest of his life prized the hymn as a precious possession. It appeared in Rippon's *Selection* in 1787.

TUNE: The tune, "Alleluia (Lowe)," was written in 1868 by an English composer, Albert Lowe, who died in 1886.

50. Joy to the World! the Lord Is Come

TUNE: *"Antioch"*

ISAAC WATTS

GEORGE FREDERICK HANDEL

Under the title, "The Messiah's Coming and Kingdom," the Rev. Isaac Watts wrote the hymn, "Joy to the world! the Lord Is come," as a translation of the last five verses of Psalm 98; and, as such, it appeared in his *Psalms of David Imitated in the Language of the New Testament,* 1719. R. Bingham, in 1870, made a Latin translation of the hymn, beginning, "Laetitia in mundo! Dominus nam venit Iësus!" (See No. 174.)

TUNE: The tune, "Antioch," is an arrangement by Lowell Mason of themes, taken from George Frederick Handel's oratorio, "The Messiah." The first theme is from the chorus, "Lift up your heads." Another is from the introduction to the recitative, "Comfort ye, My people." (See No. 139.)

51. Angels, from the Realms of Glory

TUNE: *"Regent Square"*

JAMES MONTGOMERY

HENRY SMART

James Montgomery (1771-1854), the famous hymn writer, was a journalist, as well as a poet. In 1792 he joined in the publication of the *Sheffield Register.* When his partner, Gales, left England in 1794 to escape political persecution, Montgomery took from him full charge of the paper, changing its name to the *Sheffield Iris.* In the troublous era of the French Revolution and the years that followed, Montgomery's outspoken liberal sentiments involved him in serious difficulties, and twice during the first two years of the *Iris* Montgomery was cast into prison, first for reprinting in his paper a song on "The Fall of the Bastille," and next for publishing therein an account of a Sheffield riot.

It was in this paper, which he conducted for thirty-one years, that there first appeared, on Christmas Eve of 1816, the poem, "Nativity," which with some slight alterations has become our Christmas hymn, "Angels, from the realms of glory," addressing in turn angels, shepherds, sages, saints and sinners.

TUNE: "Regent Square" by Henry Smart. (See No. 7.)

52. Fairest Lord Jesus

TUNE: *"Crusader's Hymn"*

From the German   Arranged by RICHARD S. WILLIS

"Schönster Herr Jesus" is the first line of a German hymn, which in some hymnals is annotated as "Crusader's Hymn of the 12th Century." But the evidence for such antiquity for this hymn is so slender that Julian insists that it cannot be traced further back than 1677, where in the *Münster Gesang Buch* it appears as the first of "Three beautiful selected new Hymns," its author unknown, as well as its translator into our beautiful and simple English version, "Fairest Lord Jesus."

TUNE: Likewise the tune, "Crusader's Hymn," at one time supposed to have come down from the days of the Crusades, cannot be traced farther back than 1842. It is evidently of German origin. The present arrangement was made by Richard S. Willis (1819-1900), a brother of the American poet, Nathaniel P. Willis. He was graduated from Yale, 1841, and made both music and literature his profession. He wrote much on musical topics and edited the New York *Musical World*.

53. All My Heart This Night Rejoices

TUNE: *"Bonn"*

PAUL GERHARDT   JOHN G. EBELING
Translated by CATHERINE WINKWORTH

In 1656 there appeared in Crüger's *Praxis Pietatis Melica* a long hymn of fifteen eight-line stanzas by Paul Gerhardt, beginning "Fröhlich soll mein Herze springen." It is so long that many of the English translations made therefrom are abridgments of the original. Miss Winkworth's free rendering, "All my heart this night rejoices," has great beauty. As it first appeared in her *Lyra Germanica,* it consisted of ten stanzas, from which our lovely Christmas hymn is a cento.

TUNE: J. G. Ebeling composed the tune called "Bonn" to the German words, "Warum sollt ich mich denn grämen," and they first appeared together in the book, *Geistliche Andachten,* 1666. It has since become happily associated with Gerhardt's Christmas hymn.

54. Hark! the Herald Angels Sing

TUNE: *"Mendelssohn"*

CHARLES WESLEY

FELIX MENDELSSOHN-BARTHOLDY

"Hark, how all the welkin rings, Glory to the King of kings," is the original first couplet of Charles Wesley's "Hymn for Christmas Day," which was first published in the Wesley's *Hymns and Sacred Poems,* 1739. In Wesley's revised text of 1743 the hymn appeared in four-line stanzas. Many alterations have been made in the text by Whitefield, 1753, Malan, 1760, and even Wesley himself; the most notable being in the first two lines (in our own version):

> Hark! the herald angels sing,
> Glory to the new-born King.

From the poetical standpoint, it is one of the finest hymns in the English language, and is almost universally found in Christian hymnals. (See No. 100.)

TUNE: Doctor Cummings, principal of the Guildhall School of Music, and organist at Waltham, England, regretted that Wesley's fine Christmas hymn during its one hundred and twenty years of use had never been linked with any one tune. In 1855 he found a tune in Mendelssohn's *Festgesang,* a work composed to commemorate the beginning of the art of printing, the second number in the book, and adapted it to Wesley's hymn. (See No. 163.)

55. O Come, All Ye Faithful

TUNE: *"Portuguese Hymn"*

Translated by FREDERICK OAKELEY

WADE'S Cantus Diversi

"Adeste fideles laeti triumphantes" is the first line of the old Latin hymn, from which Canon Frederick Oakeley made the English translation, "O come, all ye faithful, joyfully triumphant." The original Latin hymn has sometimes been ascribed to St. Bonaventura; but no evidence of his authorship of these lines appears in his writings, and the hymn was probably written by some German poet in the seventeenth century.

TUNE: The hymn, "Adeste Fideles," was sung in 1797 to the tune (called "Portuguese Hymn") in the Chapel of the Portuguese Embassy. Vincent Novello was the organist there, and he stated that it was composed by John Reading, who was organist in Winchester Cathedral from 1675 to 1681.

56. There's a Song in the Air

TUNE: *"Curran"*

JOSIAH G. HOLLAND   SHERMAN PRICE

Dr. Josiah Gilbert Holland, born in Belchertown, Massachusetts, July 24, 1819, turned aside from the practice of medicine to the art of writing. His *Timothy Titcomb's Letters,* 1858, won him an early fame. *Bitter Sweet* and *Kathrina* established his reputation as a poet. While he was editor of *Scribner's Monthly,* he wrote his tenderly beautiful Christmas carol, "There's a song in the air." It was published in his *The Marble Prophecy and Other Poems,* 1872.

TUNE: The tune, "Curran," was written in 1923 by Sherman Price, then a New York city school boy, eight years old, and was published in 1924. It was named "Curran" for his school teacher, Miss Virginia Curran.

57. Silent Night! Holy Night!

TUNE: *"Silent Night"*

JOSEPH MOHR   FRANZ GRUBER

"Stille Nacht! helige Nacht!" which has become Germany's most loved Christmas carol was written for the Christmas celebration of 1818 in Laufen, near Salzburg, by Joseph Mohr who was the assistant priest in the Roman Catholic church of that town. Our English translation was probably made in England, but was first published in this country in the Hutchins *Sunday School Hymnal,* 1871, prepared for the Sunday schools of the Protestant Episcopal Church. It has become as universally popular in America in our Christmas celebrations, as is the original version in Germany.

TUNE: The simple melody, called in this country "Silent Night," was specially written for Mohr's carol by Franz Gruber, who when it was composed was schoolmaster in the village of Arnsdorf, not far from Mohr's native city of Salzburg. Later he became organist in Hallein, near Salzburg, which position he held until his death in 1863.

58. As With Gladness Men of Old

TUNE: *"Dix"*

WILLIAM C. DIX   Arranged from CONRAD KOCHER

William Chatterton Dix (1837-1898), son of a surgeon in Bristol, England, was convalescing from an illness in 1860, when he wrote the hymn, "As with gladness men of old." It was first published in *Hymns of Love and Joy,* a small group of hymns, privately printed; but it soon afterwards found its way into the great hymnal of the Church of England, *Hymns Ancient and Modern,* which has had a circulation of over 60,000,000 copies, and still later into many standard hymnals throughout the English-speaking world.

TUNE: "Dix" was composed by a famous German musician, Conrad Kocher, who wrote operas, piano compositions and many songs. The melody, first published in 1838, was set to the hymn, "As with gladness," in *Hymns Ancient and Modern,* 1861, and was named for William C. Dix, the author of those lines. (See No. 3.)

59. Saw You Never in the Twilight

TUNE: *"Advent"*

MRS. CECIL F. ALEXANDER   BERTHOLD TOURS

Miss Cecil Frances Humphreys, daughter of Major John Humphreys of Tyrone, Ireland, in 1850 was married to

33

Bishop W. Alexander of Derry and Raphoe. Her fame, based on nearly four hundred hymns and poems which she wrote, has outlived that of her distinguished husband. In 1853 she wrote "Saw you never in the twilight," the year which brought the publication of her *Narrative Hymns for Village Schools*. James Davidson says: "It is as a writer for children that she has excelled."

TUNE: Berthold Tours, composer of the tune, "Advent," was a Dutch composer, born, 1838, in Rotterdam; but after musical study in Brussels and Leipzig he achieved most of his musical career in London, England, where he settled in 1861 and wrote much church music. The tune derives its title, "Advent," from the theme of the hymn. From 1878 until his death, 1897, he was musical editor of the Novello Company in London.

60.   O Little Town of Bethlehem

TUNE: *"St. Louis"*

PHILLIPS BROOKS   LEWIS H. REDNER

The Rev. Dr. Phillips Brooks, who afterwards became a bishop in the Protestant Episcopal Church, wrote in 1868 the Christmas carol for the Sunday school in the Church of the Advent, Philadelphia, of which he was then the rector. It was composed just before Christmas; and as it was on the theme of Christ's birth and his birthplace, Bethlehem, it was reminiscent in his mind of a visit he had made, two Christmases before, to the "little town of Bethlehem," where he had worshipped in the old church near the very spot where Jesus was born, and seemed to

Hear the Christmas angels
The great glad tidings tell.

TUNE: Many musical settings have been made of "O little town of Bethlehem," but the first was composed by Lewis H. Redner, organist in Doctor Brooks's Church of the Advent at the time when the hymn was written. Before retiring, one night, Redner had been reciting the poem with the idea of finding a tune for it. In the middle of the night he awoke and realized that a tune for the words was singing through his mind: he

34

arose and, striking a light, wrote out the melody on a piece of music paper, and next morning he harmonized it about as it appears in our hymnals.

61. The King of Love My Shepherd Is

TUNE: *"Dominus Regit Me"*

HENRY W. BAKER

JOHN B. DYKES

Sir Henry William Baker, eldest son of Admiral Sir Henry Loraine Baker, took holy orders in 1844, and in 1851 became the Vicar of Monkland. Of the many hymns he wrote, the first was "Oh! what if we are Christ's," and probably the most beautiful was this stirring translation of the Twenty-third Psalm, "The King of Love my Shepherd is." It was first published in *Hymns Ancient and Modern* of which Sir Henry was one of the most active editors, devoting arduous labors to make it the foremost hymnal in the world. Four of the melodies in that book were composed by him. Julian tells us that "the last audible words which lingered on his dying lips were the third stanza of his exquisite rendering of the Twenty-third Psalm, 'The King of Love my Shepherd is':

> Perverse and foolish oft I strayed,
>   But yet in love He sought me,
> And on His Shoulder gently laid,
>   And home, rejoicing, brought me."

TUNE: The music, to which this is sung, composed by the Rev. John Bacchus Dykes, has had much to do with the popularity of the hymn, so exquisitely has it interpreted the feeling of these lines. The Latin title of the tune, "Dominus Regit Me,"—"The Master rules me" —is derived from the central thought of the psalm. (See No. 113.)

62. What Grace, O Lord, and Beauty Shone

TUNE: *"Belmont"*

EDWARD DENNY

W. GARDINER

Sir Edward Denny, son of Sir E. Denny, fourth baronet of Tralee Castle, County Kerry, fell heir to his father's title in 1831. He published many hymns and poems and prose books. He was an active member of the Plymouth Brethren, and it was in their hymn-books that his hymn, "What grace, O Lord, and beauty shone," found its first wide acceptance. It was first printed, however, in Denny's *Selection of Hymns,* 1839.

TUNE: The tune, "Belmont," is often attributed to William Gardiner of Leicester, England, editor of *Sacred Melodies,* 1812; but the evidence that he composed it is very scanty. He was a stocking manufacturer, an enthusiastic musician, and in his old age published his musical reminiscences.

63.   Ye Fair Green Hills of Galilee

TUNE: *"Melita"*

EUSTACE R. CONDER   JOHN B. DYKES

The Rev. Dr. Eustace R. Conder was a Congregational clergyman, first in Poole, Dorset, England, and later at East Parade Chapel, Leeds. His first college years were spent at Spring Hill College, Birmingham: he received his Master of Arts degree at the University of London, 1844, and Doctorate of Divinity from the University of Edinburgh, 1882. It was while he was minister in Leeds that he wrote for a children's service in his church "Ye fair green hills of Galilee," which was first published in the English *Congregational Church Hymnal,* 1887, five years before his death.

TUNE: Doctor Dykes's tune, "Melita," was not written for these words, but is usually associated with Whiting's hymn of the sea, "Eternal Father, strong to save," which probably suggested the title of the tune through Paul's adventure on the Island of Melita. It was first published in *Hymns Ancient and Modern.* (See No. 113.)

64.   Majestic Sweetness Sits Enthroned

TUNE: *"Ortonville"*

SAMUEL STENNETT   THOMAS HASTINGS

The Rev. Dr. Samuel Stennett's grandfather, Joseph Stennett (1663-1713), was the first distinguished Baptist writer of English hymns. But the grandson's hymns have far outshone those of the grandfather, and a large number of them (written in the eighteenth century) are still in common use. From his hymn, "To Christ, the Lord, let every tongue," has been taken our hymn, "Majestic sweetness sits enthroned," which line began the third stanza of the original hymn. Stennett, after serving ten years as assistant to his father, who was pastor of the Little Wild Street Baptist Church in Lincoln's Inn Fields, England, succeeded him in the pastorate of that church. He had great influence with the foremost statesmen of his day. John Howard was a member of his congregation. His influence was constantly exerted toward greater religious freedom.

TUNE: "Ortonville" is one of the most popular tunes written by the American composer, Thomas Hastings. (See No. 43.)

65.   We May Not Climb the Heavenly Steeps

TUNE: *"Serenity"*

JOHN G. WHITTIER   WILLIAM V. WALLACE

The hymns, "We may not climb the heavenly steeps" and "It may not be our lot to wield," are both centos, taken from John G. Whittier's poem, "Our Master," which begins with the line, "Immortal love, for ever full." Julian has thus commented upon this: "The use of these centos shows that the hymnic element in the original poem is of a high and enduring order." The whole poem was first published in Whittier's book, *The Panorama, and Other Poems,* 1856. Whittier was known as "the Quaker poet." His hymns first found acceptance among American Unitarians, but have since passed into many evangelical hymnals. (See No. 2.)

TUNE: "Serenity" was composed by William Vincent Wallace (1814-1865), a composer of many operas, who lived a life of varied experiences. He began his musical career as a boy, leading an orchestra in Dublin, Ireland. In London he won fame as a musician, but also sorrow in his domestic relations. He then roamed through Australia,

India, and South America, spent fourteen years in Germany, lost a fortune in New York and again in London, and died in France.

66. How Sweet the Name of Jesus Sounds

TUNE: *"Holy Cross"*

JOHN NEWTON   Arranged by JAMES C. WADE

John Newton, godless sailor, African slave-trader, sea-captain, was converted first through the awful experience of facing death while steering a water-logged vessel, one stormy night, and later through his association with Whitefield and Wesley. After long study in preparation, he entered the ministry and became curate of Olney, Bucks., England, in 1764. Here he became associated with the devout English poet, William Cowper; and both of them wrote many hymns, which were published under the title, *Olney Hymns,* 1779. Here first appeared the hymn, "How sweet the name of Jesus sounds," which John Wesley, in 1781, published in his *Arminian Magazine.* It is one of the finest hymns in the English language, and among Newton's hymns is second only to "Glorious things of thee are spoken."

TUNE: "Holy Cross" was arranged by James C. Wade, an English composer of vocal music and an editor, who was born in 1847.

67. Ride On, Ride On in Majesty

TUNE: *"Winchester New"*

HENRY H. MILMAN   MUSIKALISCH HANDBUCH

It was to the brilliant young poet, Henry H. Milman, son of the famous Court physician, Sir Francis Milman, that Reginald Heber appealed to write hymns of a genuine poetic quality, when Heber was preparing a hymnal of literary as well as spiritual worth. Milman had won the poetry prize at Oxford with his *Apollo Belvidere* in 1812, which Dean Stanley called "the most perfect of Oxford prize poems." And in 1821 he became Poetry Professor at Oxford (and was succeeded, ten years later, by John

Keble). Before he had been in that chair two years, he had written the thirteen hymns of his which appeared in Heber's posthumous hymnal. His high literary standard is well sustained in his Palm Sunday hymn, "Ride on, ride on in majesty." It is a fit companion for his Good Friday hymn, "Bound on the accursed tree."

TUNE: The composer of "Winchester New" is not known; it was originally found in a German hymnal, *Musikalisch Handbuch.*

68. 'Tis Midnight; and on Olives' Brow

TUNE: *"Olives' Brow"*

WILLIAM B. TAPPAN   WILLIAM B. BRADBURY

William Bingham Tappan, born in Beverly, Massachusetts, October 29, 1794, started his career as a clock-maker in Boston at the age of sixteen; five years later entered business at Philadelphia; and seven years after that became Superintendent of the American Sunday School Union. At the age of forty-six he entered the Congregational ministry. Nine years later he died of cholera in West Needham, Massachusetts. His hymn, " 'Tis midnight; and on Olives' brow," entitled "Gethsemane," was first published, 1822, in his book, *Poems,* which was the second of ten published volumes of verse from his pen.

TUNE: The tune, "Olives' Brow," written for Tappan's hymn on that theme, and deriving its title from his first line, was composed by William B. Bradbury. (See No. 325.)

69. In the Cross of Christ I Glory

TUNE: *"Rathbun"*

JOHN BOWRING   ITHAMAR B. CONKEY

There is current an apochryphal story on the origin of "In the cross of Christ I glory," which cannot be believed. It has been told that Sir John Bowring, who became famous as the British Governor of Hongkong, was shown on his first visit to Macao the ruins of a church, destroyed by an earthquake, but with the tower still standing, surmounted by a cross; and that this scene inspired the writing of the lines, "In the cross of Christ I glory, Towering o'er the wrecks of time." But the hymn was first published in his *Hymns,* 1825, when he, thirty-two years old, was editor of the *Westminster Review,* and before he ever visited the Orient. It is remarkable that so fine a hymn on the cross should have been penned by a Unitarian. It is based on Galatians 6, 14. Sir John became eminent as the author of eight prose works, besides his many poems and hymns, and also as an outstanding British diplomat. He lived to be over eighty years old, and died on November 23, 1872.

TUNE: Ithamar B. Conkey (1815-1867), born in Shutesbury, Massachusetts, was a bass singer and a choir leader, chiefly in New York city churches. In 1847 he composed the tune, "Rathbun," to Doctor Muhlenburg's hymn, "Saviour, who Thy flock art feeding"; and in 1851 they were published together in *Collection of Church Music* by H. W. Greatorex, 1851.

70. O Sacred Head, Now Wounded
TUNE: *"Munich"*

Translated by J. W. ALEXANDER
Arranged by FELIX MENDELSSOHN BARTHOLDY

"Salve mundi salutare" is the first line of the long, ancient Latin hymn, sometimes ascribed to Bernard of Clairvaux. There seems to be little evidence, however, of his authorship. It was entitled "A rhythmical prayer to any of the members of Christ, suffering and hanging on the Cross." Its seven parts are addressed, respectively, to Christ's feet, knees, hands, side, breast, heart and face. The seventh part begins with the line, "Salve caput cruentatum." Paul Gerhardt in 1656 published a free translation of this part in German, beginning, "O Haupt voll Blut und Wunden," under the title, "To the suffering Face of Jesus Christ." Our beautifully sad hymn, "O sacred Head, now wounded," is a translation from the German into English, made by the Rev. James W. Alexander, a native of Virginia (1804), a graduate and professor of Princeton University, and a Presbyterian minister. It was first published in the *Christian Lyre,*

1830. Thus, the hymn, uttered in three tongues, represents three different churches, the Catholic (Latin), the Lutheran (German), and the Reformed (English).

TUNE: "Munich" is an old, traditional German chorale, arranged by Mendelssohn. (See No. 163.)

71. When I Survey the Wondrous Cross
TUNE: "Hamburg"
ISAAC WATTS   LOWELL MASON

Many have regarded Isaac Watts's hymn, "When I survey the wondrous cross," as the greatest English hymn. In his *Hymns and Spiritual Songs,* 1707, where it first appeared, the opening couplet is given thus:

> When I survey the wond'rous Cross
> Where the young Prince of Glory dy'd.

It was headed with the legend, "Crucifixion to the World, by the Cross of Christ," and the scriptural reference, Gal. 6, 14. The Rev. Duncan Campbell of Edinburgh has said of it: "For tender, solemn beauty, for a reverent setting forth of what the inner vision discerns as it looks upon the Crucified, I know of no verse in hymnology equal to the stanza beginning:

> See from His head, His hands, His feet,
> Sorrow and love flow mingled down." (See No. 174.)

TUNE: The melody of Lowell Mason's hymn-tune, "Hamburg," has come down to us from the ancient Gregorian music, than which probably no more worshipful music has ever been uttered in Christian churches. (See No. 21.)

72. Easter Flowers Are Blooming Bright
TUNE: "Glory in the Highest"
MARY A. NICHOLSON   FREDERICK A. G. OUSELEY

Mary A. Nicholson wrote her hymn, "Easter flowers are blooming bright," in 1875.

TUNE: The Rev. Sir Frederick A. Gore Ouseley, composer of the hymn-tune, "Glory in the Highest," in 1854 founded St. Michael's College, at Tenbury, Worcestershire, England; and in 1857 he secured as organist at the college

John Stainer, who later became famous as a hymn-tune composer. In 1889 Stainer succeeded Ouseley as Professor of Music at Oxford. Their common interest in hymn-tunes was mutually stimulating.

73. Come, Ye Faithful, Raise the Strain

Tune: *"St. Kevin"*

JOHN OF DAMASCUS   ARTHUR S. SULLIVAN
Translated by JOHN M. NEALE

John of Damascus, who flamed in the eighth century, has long been regarded as the greatest poet of the Greek Church, as well as one of the foremost theologians of all the ages of that ancient communion. The Rev. John Mason Neale (1818-1866), the great translator of Greek and Latin hymns during the first years of the Oxford Movement in the Church of England, found in the hymns of John of Damascus material for some of his best translated hymns, which he used chiefly as centos, but in the case of "Come, ye faithful, raise the strain," rendered the form as well as the spirit of John's hymn more literally than in any of his other hymns. It is replete with reference to Bible lands, where John lived nearly all of his long life, and to the glad spirit of the resurrection truth in which his mind and heart continually dwelt. (See No. 108.)

TUNE: Sir Arthur S. Sullivan (1842-1900), composer of "St. Kevin" and many others of our best hymn-tunes, became best known as composer of operettas ("Pinafore," "Mikado," "Pirates of Penzance," "Iolanthe"), though he wrote also four operas, three oratorios, three cantatas, and much instrumental and church music. He also edited *Church Hymns,* 1872. He was a London organist and conductor of choruses and orchestras.

74. Welcome, Happy Morning

Tune: *"Baptiste"*

VENANTIUS FORTUNATUS   JOHN B. CALKIN
Translated by JOHN ELLERTON

Fortunatus, author of the Latin hymn from which was translated our Easter song, "Welcome, happy morning," born in Treviso, Italy, about 531, has well been called "the last of the classics, the first of the Troubadors." His gay, happy disposition is reflected in the hymns we have derived from his Latin poetry. He was neither a bad man, nor a holy man; a poet in spite of his barbaric Latin; and some of his hymns, already nearly fourteen hundred years old, are likely to live on through the ages. Some one has said that he was "the first of the Christian poets to begin the worship of the Virgin Mary, which rose to a passion and sank to an idolatry." Denatured of objectionable Roman doctrines, his hymns find wide favor among Protestants, especially his "The royal banners forward go" and "Welcome, happy morning." (See No. 33.)

TUNE: The tune, "Baptiste," derived its title from the middle name of its composer, John Baptiste Calkins. He was an English organist, born in London, 1827, studied in St. Columba's College, Ireland, and in Woburn and London. In 1899 he was made professor at Guildhall School. He wrote much church music, instrumental pieces and part-songs, and some very effective hymn-tunes. He died in 1905.

75. Christ the Lord Is Risen Today

TUNE: *"Easter Hymn"*

CHARLES WESLEY   *Lyra Davidica*

"Christ our Lord is risen today" (to quote the first line, as it is sometimes rendered) has become one of the most popular of the six thousand hymns that came from the facile pen of the greatest of English hymn-writers, Charles Wesley. It first appeared in the Wesley's *Hymns and Sacred Poems,* 1739, under the title, "Hymn for Easter"; was strangely omitted by John Wesley from his *Wesleyan Hymn Book,* 1780; but has since passed into almost universal use for the time of Easter. (See No. 100.)

TUNE: The hymn-tune, "Easter Hymn," is found first in a small tune-book, *Lyra Davidica,* 1708; but its composer is unknown. A copy of the book is in the British Museum.

76. The Day of Resurrection

TUNE: *"Rotterdam"*

JOHN OF DAMASCUS   BERTHOLD TOURS
Translated by JOHN M. NEALE

"The day of resurrection" is another great hymn which the Rev. Dr. John Mason Neale translated from the Greek lines of John of Damascus. (See No. 73.) The original Greek hymn is still used by the Greek Church in their Easter Sabbath worship throughout the world: in fact, the singing of this glad paean of joy is rarely ever omitted by them in their Easter morning services. (See No. 108.)

TUNE: The title of the tune, "Rotterdam," one of the cities of Holland, is reminiscent of the fact that its composer, Berthold Tours, was born in Holland; although it was composed during his musical career in London. (See No. 59.)

77. Look, Ye Saints, the Sight Is Glorious

TUNE: *"Regent Square"*

THOMAS KELLY   HENRY SMART

"And He shall reign for ever, and ever" was the title of the hymn, "Look, ye saints, the sight is glorious." It was published first in the Rev. Thomas Kelly's *Hymns on Various Passages of Scripture,* 1809. Kelly, the son of an Irish judge, was born in Dublin, 1769, was graduated from Trinity College, Dublin, began as a lawyer, but in 1792 entered the ministry of the Established Church, from which he later seceded to become an independent minister. Of his 765 hymns, many are of a very high order, as is witnessed by this brilliant hymn on the second coming of Christ.

TUNE: "Regent Square" (See No. 7).

78. All Hail the Power of Jesus' Name

. TUNES: *"Coronation"*; *"Miles Lane"*

                    OLIVER HOLDEN
EDWARD PERRONET   WILLIAM SHRUBSOLE

The Rev. Edward Perronet, who wrote the famous hymn, "All hail the power of Jesus' name," was born in England, 1726, though of French ancestry. Brought up in the

Church of England, he savagely revolted from its doctrines and methods, and became an evangelical preacher under Wesley. But soon he broke with the Wesleys, joined the Countess of Huntingdon's Connexion, and eventually became a Congregational minister at Canterbury. He wrote many fine hymns, none more popular than "All hail the power of Jesus' name," which first appeared in the November issue of the *Gospel Magazine,* 1779.

FIRST TUNE: "Miles Lane," by William Shrubsole, was printed in connection with the hymn, "All hail the power," when it was first published in the *Gospel Magazine,* 1779, though not under that title. William Shrubsole (1752-1806) was first a chorister in Canterbury Cathedral, and later organist in Spafields Chapel, London.

SECOND TUNE: "Coronation" was composed by Oliver Holden, who was born in Shirley, Massachusetts, on September 18, 1765, and was first published in his book, *The Union Harmony or Universal Collection of Sacred Music,* 1793. He edited also the *Worcester Collection* and composed a score of hymn-tunes. He died in 1844. (See No. 194.)

79. The Head That Once Was Crowned With Thorns

TUNE: *"Neidlinger"*

THOMAS KELLY

WILLIAM NEIDLINGER

Another of the *Hymns on Various Passages of Scripture* by the Rev. Thomas Kelly is "The Head that once was crowned with thorns." (See No. 77.) It appeared in the edition of 1820, and is based on Hebrews 2, 10. H. M. Macgill in his *Songs of the Christian Creed and Life,* 1876, has rendered it into Latin, the first line being, "Spinis caput coronatum."

TUNE: William Neidlinger, organist of St. Michael's Church, New York city, composed his tune (which the publishers have named for him "Neidlinger") in 1924 to the words of the Harvard Prize Hymn by the late Rev. Harry Webb Farrington, "I know not how that Bethlehem's Babe." It was first published in 1925 in *Hymns of the Christian Life,* set to these words.

45

80. Crown Him With Many Crowns

TUNE: *"Diademata"*

MATTHEW BRIDGES   GEORGE J. ELVEY

There are four well-known hymns that begin with the first line, "Crown Him with many crowns." This hymn by Matthew Bridges, an English author (born in Essex, 1800), who later lived in Canada, was contained in *Hymns of the Heart,* second edition, 1851, with the Latin title, "In capite ejus diademata multa. Apoc. 19, 12." In the *Passion of Jesus* by Bridges, 1852, the title is "Third Sorrowful Mystery, Song of the Seraphs."

TUNE: Sir George Job Elvey, born at Canterbury, England, 1816, was a famous organist (for 47 years at Windsor), choral conductor, and composer of two oratorios and much choral music. He received his degree, Mus. Doc., from Oxford, 1840; and was knighted, 1871. His hymn-tune, "Diademata," takes its title from the Latin word for "crowns," thus linking it with Bridges' hymn, "Crown him with many crowns." Elvey died at Windsor, England, 1893.

81. Holy Ghost, With Light Divine

TUNE: *"Mercy"*

ANDREW REED   LOUIS M. GOTTSCHALK
                               Arranged by EDWIN P. PARKER

The Rev. Dr. Andrew Reed was the Congregational pastor, first of the New Road Chapel, St. George's-in-the-East, and later of Wycliffe Chapel, London. Philanthropic in his impulses, he founded the London Orphan Asylum, the Asylum for Fatherless Children, the Asylum for Idiots, the Infant Orphan Asylum and the Hospital for Incurables. About a dozen of his hymns are in common use, the best known being this "Prayer to the Holy Spirit," written in 1817, and beginning, "Holy Ghost, with light divine." The words, "shine," "cleanse," "dwell," "reign," note the development of the work of the Holy Spirit in the soul.

TUNE: The tune, "Mercy," was arranged by the Rev. Dr. Edwin P. Parker (see No. 160) from a well-known piano piece by Louis Moreau Gottschalk, entitled "Last Hope." Gottschalk was an American pianist of some distinction and a composer especially of piano pieces. He died, 1869, at the age of forty.

82. Come, Holy Ghost, in Love

TUNE: *"New Haven"*

Translated by RAY PALMER

THOMAS HASTINGS

There is a great doubt as to the authorship of the Latin hymn, "Veni, Sancte Spiritus," from which the Rev. Dr. Ray Palmer translated his hymn, "Come, Holy Ghost, in love." It is known as the Golden Sequence, an example of the revival of interest in rhymed hymns which was fostered by Adam of St. Victor. Its double and triple rhymes in the original Latin are ingenious and beautiful. It has been attributed to King Robert of France, Pope Innocent III, Hermanus Contractus, and Archbishop Langton; but for none of these does the evidence available yield a clear title to the authorship. (See No. 126, on Ray Palmer.)

TUNE: Dr. Thomas Hastings's tune, "New Haven," is named for the leading town in his native state of Connecticut.. (See No. 43.)

83. Spirit of God, Descend Upon My Heart

TUNE: *"Morecambe"*

GEORGE CROLY

FREDERICK C. ATKINSON

The Rev. Dr. George Croly was born in Dublin, Ireland, 1780, and was educated in Dublin University. After serving in the ministry in Ireland for some years, in 1810 he came to London and followed a literary career. His deeply spiritual hymn on the Holy Spirit, "Spirit of God, descend upon my heart," was included in his *Psalms and Hymns for Public Worship*, London, 1854.

TUNE: The tune, "Morecambe," was composed by Frederick Cook Atkinson, an English organist and composer, who was born August 21, 1841. He studied music under Dr. Z. Buck, received his degree, Mus. Bac., from

Cambridge University, became the organist in Manningham Church, Bradford, and Norwich Cathedral, and composed many anthems, services and songs.

84. O for That Flame of Living Fire

TUNE: *"Melcombe"*

WILLIAM H. BATHURST   SAMUEL WEBBE

The Rev. William Hiley Bathurst had the courage of his convictions and much of the flaming spirit which he utters in his hymn, "O for that flame of living fire." An Oxford graduate, 1818, he became rector of Barwick-in-Elmet, near Leeds, England, which post he held from 1820 until 1852. But when he found that he could not reconcile his convictions with the doctrines expressed in the Book of Common Prayer, he withdrew from the Church of England; and the last fifteen years of his life he spent in retirement.

TUNE: The tune, "Melcombe," is taken from a *Collection of Motets* by Samuel Webbe, which was published in 1791. It was there set to the Latin hymn, "O salutaris hostia." Webbe, a Roman Catholic composer, wrote various settings of the mass, from which hymn-tunes have been derived. He was born in Minorca, 1740, and died in London, 1816, where for years he had been organist in the Sardinian Chapel, and where he edited and composed a large body of music, chiefly anthems and songs, for which he received twenty-six medals.

85. Gracious Spirit, Dwell With Me

TUNE: *"Fingest"*

THOMAS TOKE LYNCH   J. A. MAUNDERS

The Rivulet: a Contribution to Sacred Song, London, 1855, is the title of a collection of original hymns which the Rev. Thomas T. Lynch wrote for the use of his congregation in Mortimer Street, London, afterwards at Grafton Street, Fitzroy Square. The appearance of this book, which contained among other hymns his "Gracious Spirit, dwell with me," created such a bitter controversy on account of its subjective quality that it practically divided the Congregationalists of England into two parties. The hymn, however, has survived the controversy, and is becoming increasingly popular. (See No. 24.)

TUNE: John A. Maunders, composer of the tune, "Fingest," was born in Chelsea, England, 1858, became an organist and composed church cantatas, anthems, etc. He died in 1920.

86. Our Blest Redeemer, Ere He Breathed

TUNE: *"Wreford"*

HARRIET AUBER   EDMUND S. CARTER

Miss Harriet Auber, an English poet, rendered a beautiful service to devotional poetry when she published in 1829 her book, *Spirit of the Psalms.* Many of the hymns and metrical psalms therein have been used in modern hymnals; but none more frequently than her hymn on Whitsuntide, "Our blest Redeemer." It has been translated into many languages and is sung throughout the world.

TUNE: The composer of the tune, "Wreford," was the Rev. Edmund Sardinson Carter, an English clergyman, who was born in 1845.

87. A Glory Gilds the Sacred Page

TUNE: *"Manoah"*

WILLIAM COWPER   From FRANCIS J. HAYDN

William Cowper's "A glory gilds the sacred page" is entitled "The Light and Glory of the Word" in *Olney Hymns,* 1779. It is eloquent of his own personal experience. He tells us that the text, Romans 3, 24, "Being justified freely by his grace, through the redemption that is in Christ Jesus," *et seq.,* brought about his conversion one day in July, 1764, at the St. Alban's Asylum. Thereafter for him there was always a glory gilding the sacred page. (See No. 114.)

TUNE: "Manoah" is based on a melody, taken from the works of Francis J. Haydn, the world-famous composer. (See No. 17.)

88. O Word of God Incarnate

TUNE: *"Aurelia"*

WILLIAM WALSHAM HOW   SAMUEL S. WESLEY

Bishop William W. How of the Church of England, who was first Bishop of Bedford, and later Bishop of Wakefield (1888), was author of many prose volumes on scriptural and ecclesiastical themes; but his fame will live rather in many of the hymns he has given to the church, rich in ideas, simple and direct in expression, and spiritually practical. His hymn on the Holy Scriptures, "O Word of God incarnate," was written for the supplement of 1867 to Morrell and How's *Psalms and Hymns.* The bishop died in 1897.

TUNE: Samuel Sebastian Wesley (1810-1876), grandson of the great hymn-writer, Charles Wesley, was organist in Hereford and Exeter, Winchester and Gloucester Cathedrals. He edited *The European Psalmist,* 1872. He was a prolific writer of church music, including many of our best hymn-tunes. One of these, "Aurelia," he published to the hymn, "Jerusalem the golden," in *A Selection of Psalms and Hymns Arranged for the Public Service of the Church of England* by the Rev. Charles Kemble, 1864. Its title, "Aurelia," is the Latin word for "golden," and refers to the first line of the hymn, "Jerusalem the golden."

89. Thy Word Is Like a Garden, Lord

TUNE: *"Seraph"*

EDWIN HODDER   Old English Melody

Edwin Hodder, born in Staines, Middlesex, England, 1837, went to New Zealand before he became of age. On his return to England in 1861, he entered the English Civil Service. Two years later, he brought out *The New Sunday School Hymn Book,* which contained his hymn on the Scriptures, "Thy Word is like a garden, Lord." His similes, expressed each in one of the four quatrains of the first two stanzas, picture the Word of God as a garden, a mine, a constellation of stars, an armory. The final stanza gathers these poetical pictures into a prayer that the singer may realize in his life the strength and beauty of the Word.

TUNE: "Seraph" is an English folk melody, popular in the seventeenth century.

90. Glorious Things of Thee Are Spoken
TUNE: "Austria"

JOHN NEWTON

FRANCIS J. HAYDN

"Glorious things of thee are spoken" is the finest of the Rev. John Newton's hymns. It was published in *Olney Hymns,* 1779, under the title, "Zion; or the City of God," and is based on Psalms 87, 3, "Glorious things are spoken of thee, O city of God," and upon Isaiah 33, 20-21. Many have compared Newton's hymns unfavorably with those of his hymnic collaborator, William Cowper. But Lord Selborne speaks more justly of the manliness of Newton and the tenderness of Cowper. Surely Cowper wrote no finer hymn than this splendid song of praise. (See No. 66.)

TUNE: The hymn-tune, "Austria," is one of the very few melodies especially composed for a national hymn. Francis Joseph Haydn (see No. 17) wrote it for the Austrian national hymn that had been written by Hauschka, and it was first publicly rendered on the birthday of the Austrian Emperor, February 12, 1797. It was first published as a hymn-tune in Miller's collection of tunes to Watts's *Psalms and Hymns Set to Music,* 1805.

91. Oh! Where Are Kings and Empires Now
TUNE: "St. Anne"

A. CLEVELAND COXE

WILLIAM CROFT

Bishop Arthur Cleveland Coxe was born in Mendham, New Jersey, May 10, 1818. After serving as rector of Protestant Episcopal churches in Hartford and Baltimore, he became in 1868 the Bishop of Buffalo. The year after his graduation from New York University, *The Churchman* published his ballad, "Chelsea," from the sixth stanza of which begins his hymn, "Oh! where are kings and empires now." He was but twenty years old when he wrote these stately lines upon the Church of God.

TUNE: When in London, England, an organ was built in St. Anne's Church, Soho, 1700, William Croft was chosen to be organist, and this association gave the title to his hymn-tune, "St. Anne." As organist later of the Royal Chapel and of Westminster Abbey, and as the composer of many anthems, songs and instrumental pieces, he became recognized as one of the foremost musicians in London, and received from Oxford University the degree of Doctor of Music. He was born in Nether Ettington, Warwickshire, 1678, and died in Bath, 1727. He was buried in Westminster Abbey, where a monument commemorates his fame.

92.   I Love Thy Kingdom, Lord

TUNE: *"St. Thomas"*

TIMOTHY DWIGHT   Aaron Williams Collection

In 1785 Joel Barlow, a popular American literary figure in his generation, made a revision of Isaac Watts's metrical psalms. But this was so unsatisfactory to American congregations that in 1797 the General Association asked the Rev. Dr. Timothy Dwight, who had then been President of Yale College for two years, to make an entirely new revision of Watts. This he did, and the result was published in a memorable volume in 1800. The hymn, "I love Thy kingdom, Lord," which is Doctor Dwight's third version of Psalm 137, is the most popular memento we have of that collection. In some of the Scottish and Irish hymnals the hymn opens with what is our second stanza.

TUNE: Aaron Williams (1731-1776), to whom the tune, "St. Thomas," is often attributed, was born in England of Welsh parentage. He composed many psalm-tunes, was a teacher, engraver and publisher of music in London. He edited *The Universal Psalmodist,* before 1766, *The Royal Harmony,* 1766, and *Universal Psalmodist,* 1769.

93.   The Church's One Foundation

TUNE: *"Aurelia"*

SAMUEL J. STONE   SAMUEL S. WESLEY

The curate of Windsor, England, the Rev. Samuel J. Stone, was so stirred by an attack upon the faith of his church, begun by Bishop John W. Colenso, that he wrote a series of twelve hymns upon the points of the Apostles' Creed. On the ninth article, "The Holy Catholic Church, the communion of saints," he composed this hymn, "The church's one foundation is Jesus Christ the Lord," and set forth in these lines his belief in the church as Christ's holy bride, His creation, His redeemed. (See No. 270.)

TUNE: "Aurelia" (See No. 88).

94. See Israel's Gentle Shepherd Stand

TUNE: *"Serenity"*

PHILIP DODDRIDGE

WILLIAM V. WALLACE

"Christ's condescending Regard to little Children" is the title of the Rev. Dr. Philip Doddridge's hymn, "See Israel's gentle Shepherd stand," which was not published until after his death, when in 1755 Job Orton included it in a posthumous volume of Doddridge's *Hymns*. Doddridge (1702-1751) was a contemporary and friend of Whitefield and the Wesleys, the writer of nearly four hundred published hymns, a non-conformist pastor of a large group of young men who entered the Christian ministry.

TUNE: "Serenity" (See No. 65).

95. The King of Heaven His Table Spreads

TUNE: *"Dundee"*

PHILIP DODDRIDGE

Scotch Psalter

Another hymn from Doctor Doddridge's pen, "The Gospel Feast," is the widely used communion service invitation hymn, "The King of heaven His table spreads." The author was accustomed to write many of his hymns after church worship on the main theme of his sermon that day. The hallowed spirit of the Holy Communion which he had just administered is reproduced in the tender lines of this hymn. (See No. 94.)

TUNE: The traditional Scotch tune, "Dundee," has long had a grip upon the singers of metrical psalms in Scotland. Robert Burns in his "Cotter's Saturday Night" refers to it in the line,

Perhaps Dundee's wild, warbling measures rise.

96. Jesus Spreads His Banner O'er Us

TUNE: *"Autumn"*

ROSWELL PARK

LOUIS VON ESCH

Educated at Union College and West Point, Roswell Park entered the United States Army and later became professor of Chemistry in the University of Pennsylvania. In 1843 he entered the ministry, in 1852 became President of Racine College and afterwards Chancellor. He was principal of a school in Chicago, when he died in 1869. His hymn on "Holy Communion," "Jesus spreads His banner o'er us," was written while he was in his twenties, and was published in his *Poems*, 1836.

TUNE: The tune, "Autumn," is sometimes attributed to Louis von Esch, a German composer, and sometimes to François H. Barthélemon, a French violinist and composer. (See No. 13.)

97. According to Thy Gracious Word

TUNE: *"Dalehurst"*

JAMES MONTGOMERY

ARTHUR COTTMAN

"This do in remembrance of Me" is the motto which James Montgomery (1771-1854) printed with his communion hymn, "According to Thy gracious word," when it first appeared in his *Christian Psalmist*, 1825. Curiously, no copy of this hymn has been found among Montgomery's manuscripts; but it has been reproduced in a wide range of hymnals. (See No. 51.)

TUNE: "Dalehurst" is by Arthur Cottman, the English solicitor and composer. (See No. 16.)

98. Bread of the World in Mercy Broken

TUNE: *"Eucharistic Hymn"*

REGINALD HEBER

JOHN S. B. HODGES

When Bishop Heber's hymn, "Bread of the world," was published in his posthumous *Hymns written and adapted to the Weekly Church Service of the Year*, 1827 (see No. 27), it bore the title, "Before the Sacrament." In the *Mitre Hymn Book,* the first line was changed to "Bread of our life in mercy broken"; but this alteration has not prevailed in general usage.

TUNE: The son of the distinguished English organist, Edward Hodges, was the Rev. John Sebastian Bach Hodges, rector of St. Paul's Church, Baltimore, Maryland. He inherited his father's musical interest and composed many hymn-tunes. His "Eucharistic Hymn" takes its title from the subject of Bishop Heber's hymn, to which it is set.

99. Come, Said Jesus' Sacred Voice

TUNE: *"Haven"*

ANNA L. BARBAULD

EDWARD H. LEMARE

Anna L. Aiken was the daughter of the Rev. Dr. John Aiken who taught in Warrington Academy. Here she met one of the students, Rochemont Barbauld (of French descent), and in 1774 married him. He entered the ministry, serving as pastor and teacher at the same time. While he was minister to the congregation at Hampstead, she wrote the hymn, "Come, said Jesus' sacred voice," which is but one of a number of successful hymns written by ministers' wives. It was published in 1792.

TUNE: Edwin H. Lemare, who composed the hymn-tune, "Haven," was born at Ventnor, Isle of Wight, England, in 1865. He became a distinguished organist in Sheffield and London (Holy Trinity, Sloane Street and St. Margaret's, Westminster). He toured the world as a recitalist, in America was city organist in Pittsburgh, 1902-1905; in San Francisco, 1917; in Portland, Maine, 1920. He wrote two symphonies for the organ, overtures, marches and a considerable volume of church music.

100. Depth of Mercy! Can There Be

TUNE: *"Seymour"*

CHARLES WESLEY

CARL MARIA VON WEBER

Charles Wesley's title for the hymn, "Depth of mercy! can there be," was "After a Relapse Into Sin." This is accentuated by the second line of the third stanza, wherein Wesley originally wrote "Let me now my fall lament," instead of "my *sins* lament," as it is now sung. The Wesleys' *Hymns and Sacred Poems,* 1740, gave the hymn its first publication. The Rev. Charles Wesley, brother of John Wesley, founder of Methodism, was born in Epworth, 1707, was graduated from Oxford and accompanied his brother in his missionary tour to Georgia, U. S. A. Throughout the Wesleyan revival he was the "Singer of Methodism," writing over 6,000 hymns, and, as itinerant preacher, aiding his brother in stirring the British nation from out of its spiritual lethargy. He died in 1788.

TUNE: "Seymour." (See No. 29.)

101. O Jesus, Thou Art Standing

TUNE: *"Hilda"*

WILLIAM H. HOW   JUSTIN H. KNECHT and EDWARD HUSBAND

Bishop William H. How of the Church of England (1823-1897) wrote this note concerning the origin of his hymn, "O Jesus, Thou art standing":

I composed the hymn early in 1867, after I had been reading a very beautiful poem, entitled, "Brothers and a Sermon." The pathos of the verses impressed me very forcibly at the time. I read them over and over again, and finally, closing the book, I scribbled on an odd scrap of paper my first idea of the verses, beginning, "O Jesus, Thou art standing." I altered them a good deal subsequently, but I am fortunate in being able to say that after the hymn left my hands it was never revised or altered in any way.

TUNE: Justin Heinrich Knecht, who composed the melody, from which was taken the hymn-tune, "Hilda," or "St. Hilda," as it is sometimes called, was a German composer, who was born in 1752 and died in 1817. For many years he was professor of literature at Biberbach. The Rev. Edward Husband, who adapted and modified Knecht's tune, was born in Folkestone, England, and began his career as clergyman of the Church of England in 1866, being curate of Atherstone and of Folkestone, and vicar of St. Michael and All Angels churches in Folkestone. In 1874 he published *The Mission Hymnal* in which some of his own hymns first appeared.

102. Just as I Am, Without One Plea

TUNE: *"Woodworth"*

CHARLOTTE ELLIOTT

WILLIAM B. BRADBURY

Miss Charlotte Elliott (1789-1871) lived in Clapham, England, until 1823, and thereafter at Brighton until her death. During most of her life she was an invalid; but the tender hymns she wrote in her sick-room have reached the hearts of millions; and none more completely than "Just as I am, without one plea." She wrote this one afternoon when her sisters, attending a church bazaar, left her all alone. The memory of Dr. Caesar Milan's encouraging words to her on the day she was converted— "Dear Charlotte, cut the cable, . . . you must come to Christ just as you are"—were the inspiration of the hymn. She showed it to her returning sisters, and it was published in her *Invalid's Hymn Book,* 1836, and afterwards all over the world.

TUNE: The tune, "Woodworth," by William B. Bradbury, was published in Hastings and Bradbury's hymnal, *The Third Book of Psalms,* 1849, to a hymn, "The God of love will surely indulge," by Elizabeth Scott. (See No. 325.)

103. Just as I Am, Thine Own To Be

TUNE: *"Just As I Am"*

MARIANNE HEARN

JOSEPH BARNBY

Marianne Hearn in 1887 wrote her hymn, "Just as I am, Thine own to be." It is modeled upon Charlotte Elliott's hymn, "Just as I am, without one plea," of which it is in a sense the complement, and not a parody. It is an expression of the Godward aspirations of youth, and as such is becoming increasingly popular. It was published in *The Voice of Praise,* 1887, by the Sunday School Union, London. Born in Farningham, Kent, England, 1834, Miss Hearn became a primary school teacher in Gravesend and in Northampton (1865). She was on the staff of *The Christian World* and edited *The Sunday School Times.* Her poems appeared in many volumes, and her autobiography was entitled, *A Working Woman's Life.* She died in Barmouth, 1909.

TUNE: The tune, "Just As I Am," was composed by Sir Joseph Barnby to Charlotte Elliott's hymn, "Just as I am without one plea." (See No. 14.)

104. Rock of Ages, Cleft for Me

TUNE: *"Toplady"*

AUGUSTUS M. TOPLADY   THOMAS HASTINGS

The Rev. Augustus M. Toplady (1740-1778) entered the ministry of the Church of England, 1762, but soon after joined the French Calvinists. His diatribes against the Wesleys and others opposed to Calvinism were bitter. Canon Julian says: "He was impulsive, rash-spoken, reckless in misjudgment; but a flame of genuine devoutness burned in the fragile lamp of his over-tasked and wasted body." He is remembered today for his supremely popular hymn, "Rock of Ages," which he entitled when it first appeared in his own *Gospel Magazine,* March, 1776, "A living and dying PRAYER, for the HOLIEST BE-LIEVER in the World." It has been much altered: the second line of the last stanza, for instance, was originally, "When my eye-strings break in death."

TUNE: The tune, "Toplady," was originally written to Toplady's hymn, "Rock of Ages": hence its title. (See No. 43.)

105. Jesus, Meek and Gentle

TUNE: *"Town"*

GEORGE R. PRYNNE   ROBERT G. McCUTCHAN

The Rev. George R. Prynne, born in Cornwall, England, 1818, and educated at Cambridge University, has given us this note on his hymn, "Jesus, meek and gentle":

This little hymn has found its way into most English Hymn-books. It is commonly thought to have been written for children, and on this supposition I have been asked to simplify the fourth verse. The hymn was not, however, written specially for children. Where it is used in collections of hymns for children, it might be well to alter the last two lines in the fourth verse thus:

Through earth's passing darkness,
To heaven's endless day.

TUNE: The tune, "Town," was composed by Dean Robert G. McCutchan in 1928, and was named for Dr. S. B. Town, who for years was treasurer of DePauw University and whose wonderful character and sweetness and gentleness suggested his name for that particular tune.

106. Come, Ye Sinners, Poor and Needy

TUNE: *"Greenville"*

JOSEPH HART   JEAN J. ROUSSEAU

"Come, and Welcome to Jesus Christ" was the title of the Rev. Joseph Hart's hymn, "Come, ye sinners, poor and needy," when it was first published in his *Hymns Composed on Various Subjects,* 1759. It is eloquent of his own experience; for from the attitude of a militant atheist (he once wrote "The Unreasonableness of Religion," as a reply to John Wesley's sermon on Romans 8, 32), he was converted in 1757, at the age of forty-five, to a rich religious experience, which flowered in many years of service as a Congregational clergyman.

TUNE: Jean Jacques Rousseau (1712-1778), famous philosopher, was the composer of five operas, among them being "Le Devin du Village" ("The Soothsayer of the Village") which was rendered before the King of France at Fontainebleau, October 18, 1752. A melody from this opera became a popular song, entitled "Rousseau's Dream," in the middle of the nineteenth century, and then a hymn-tune, called "Greenville," usually sung to Hart's hymn, "Come, ye sinners."

107. Weary of Earth, and Laden With My Sin

TUNE: *"Langran"*

SAMUEL J. STONE   JAMES LANGRAN

"Weary of earth" is another of the Rev. Samuel J. Stone's series of hymns on different articles of the Apostles' Creed. Just as "The church's one foundation" (see No. 93) was based on the phrase, "the Holy Catholic Church, the communion of saints," so was this hymn founded on the phrase, "the forgiveness of sins." It was written in 1866 for a parochial mission conducted by the author and printed that year in his book, *Lyra Fidelium.*

Dr. Charles S. Robinson has said that this hymn is "one of the finest in our language as an eager and wistful imploration of pardon for one's iniquities in the sight of God." (See No. 270.)

TUNE: James Langran was an English musician, who was born in 1835, and became well known in London as an organist and musical editor. His tune, "Langran," is named for him.

108. Art Thou Weary, Art Thou Languid

TUNE: *"Bullinger"*

JOHN M. NEALE   ETHELBERT W. BULLINGER

"'Art thou weary' and two other hymns contain so little that is from the Greek that they ought not to have been included in this collection." So wrote Dr. John Mason Neale in his preface to the third edition of *Hymns of the Eastern Church,* 1866, composed chiefly of translations of Greek hymns. The dominant ideas of the hymn, however, were derived from the ancient poetic lines of St. Stephen the Sabaite, who lived from 725 to 794, and was a monk at Mar Saba, near the Dead Sea of Palestine.

Doctor Neale, born in London, 1818, was graduated from Cambridge, 1840, entered the ministry, 1841, and was Warden of Sackville College, Sussex, from 1846 until his death, 1866. Stirred by the Oxford Movement in the Church of England, he unburied the ancient treasures of Greek and Latin hymnody, and through his excellent translations made them accessible to worshippers in English.

TUNE: The composer of the tune, "Bullinger," was an English clergyman of the last century, the Rev. Ethelbert W. Bullinger.

109. Come Unto Me, Ye Weary

TUNE: *"Savoy Chapel"*

WILLIAM C. DIX   JOHN B. CALKIN

William Chatterton Dix (1837-1898) once gave this account of the writing of his hymn, "Come unto Me," in 1867, which *The People's Hymnal,* London, published that same year:

I was ill and depressed at the time, and it was almost to idle away the hours that I wrote the hymn. I had been ill for many weeks, and felt weary and faint, and the hymn really expresses the languidness of body from which I was suffering at the time. Soon after its composition I recovered, and I always look back to that hymn as the turning point in my illness.

TUNE: The tune, "Savoy Chapel," was composed by John Baptiste Calkin. (See No. 74.)

110.   I Am Trusting Thee, Lord Jesus
TUNE: *"Rest, Sullivan"*
FRANCES R. HAVERGAL   ARTHUR S. SULLIVAN

Of all the hundreds of hymns which were composed by that devoutly consecrated singer, Miss Frances Ridley Havergal (1836-1879), "I am trusting Thee, Lord Jesus," was her own favorite; and after her death it was found in her pocket Bible. She wrote it at Ormont Dessons in September, 1874, and it was published in *Loyal Responses,* 1878. She also later composed the tune, "Urbane," especially for these lines. She was the daughter of a clergyman of the Church of England, the Rev. W. H. Havergal, who also was a composer of hymn-tunes.

TUNE: To distinguish this tune from another, named "Rest," by William B. Bradbury, it is here called "Rest, Sullivan," as it was composed by Sir Arthur S. Sullivan. (See No. 73.)

111.   Grace! 'Tis the Charming Sound
TUNE: *"Silver Street"*
PHILIP DODDRIDGE   ISAAC SMITH

Another hymn by the Rev. Philip Doddridge, based on one of his own sermons (from the text, Ephesians 2, 5) is "Grace! 'Tis a charming sound." The hymn has many different versions, some of them beginning with the line, "Grace! 'Tis a joyful sound"; others being centos. As printed in this hymnal, it is with slight alterations the same as the original version, first printed in Doddridge's *Hymns Founded on Various Texts in the Holy Scriptures,* published in 1755 after Doddridge's death. (See No. 94.)

TUNE: "Silver Street," sometimes called "Falcon Street" (both of them streets in London), was composed by Isaac Smith, who died about 1800. He was a director of music in a Non-conformist chapel in Goodman's Fields, London, and edited a hymnal, *Collection of Psalm Tunes.*

112. Beneath the Cross of Jesus

TUNE: *"St. Christopher"*

ELIZABETH C. CLEPHANE   FREDERICK C. MAKER

Miss Elizabeth Cecilia Clephane, third daughter of the Sheriff of Fife, Scotland, was famous for her many charities among the poor of her neighborhood in Bridgend, Melrose. She contributed regularly to *The Children's Hour.* After her death in 1869 the hymn, "Beneath the cross of Jesus," and others of her composition (including "The Ninety and Nine") were published in *The Family Treasury* under the title, "Breathings on the Border." The Rev. W. Arnot, the editor, in introducing them, wrote:

These lines express the experiences, the hopes, and the longings of a young Christian lately released. Written on the very edge of this life, with the better land fully in the view of faith, they seem to us footsteps printed on the sands of Time, where these sands touch the ocean of Eternity. These footprints of one whom the Good Shepherd led through the wilderness into rest may, with God's blessing, contribute to comfort and direct succeeding pilgrims.

TUNE: Frederick Charles Maker, who wrote the hymn-tune, "St. Christopher," was an English composer of church anthems and hymn-tunes, who was born in 1844. "Christopher" etymologically means "Bearer of Christ."

113. O Thou Whose Spirit Witness Bears

TUNE: *"St. Agnes"*

FREDERICK L. HOSMER   JOHN B. DYKES

The Rev. Frederick L. Hosmer, born in Framingham, Massachusetts, 1840, wrote his hymn, "O Thou whose Spirit," for the dedication of the First Unitarian Church in Omaha, Nebraska, on February 6, 1891. It bore the legend, "For T. K.; Omaha, 1891," when it was printed in *The Thought of God,* Second Series, 1894. Hosmer died in California in 1929. (See No. 273).

TUNE: The Rev. Dr. John Bacchus Dykes was born in Hull, England, 1823. As a boy he was organist in St.

John's Church, Hull. At Cambridge University, to which he came for an education, fortified by a scholarship won at St. Catherine's Hall, he became conductor of the University Musical Society. Entering the ministry of the Church of England, he became curate at Malton, Yorkshire, minor canon and percentor at Durham Cathedral, and then for twelve years Vicar of St. Oswald's, Durham; where he composed most of his hymn-tunes. A dispute with his bishop and its unfortunate consequences led him to retire to St. Leonard's, where soon afterwards he died, January 20, 1876. "St. Agnes" is one of his best-loved tunes.

114.   Hark, My Soul, It Is the Lord
TUNE: *"St. Bees"*

WILLIAM COWPER   JOHN B. DYKES

The English poet, William Cowper, born in his father's rectory at Berkhampstead, 1731, was educated at Westminster, was called to the Bar, 1754, lived in Huntingdon for a while, and in 1768 moved to Olney, where he developed a literary partnership with his pastor, the Rev. John Newton. They each wrote many hymns and together published the famous *Olney Hymns, 1779.* Later he lived in Weston and in East Dereham, where he died in 1800. His life was occasionally clouded by melancholy which sometimes amounted to insanity. It was during his residence at Olney that he wrote "Hark, my soul, it is the Lord," which Julian calls "a lyric of great tenderness and beauty, and ranks as one of Cowper's best hymns."

TUNE: "St. Bees," a hymn-tune by Dr. John B. Dykes, was first published in the Rev. R. R. Chope's *Congregational Hymn and Tune Book, 1862.* (See No. 113.)

115.   I Heard the Voice of Jesus Say
TUNE: *"Vox Dilecti"*

HORATIUS BONAR   JOHN B. DYKES

It was in Kelso that the Rev. Dr. Horatius Bonar (1808-1889) entered the ministry of the Established Church in 1837, and there, after joining in the "Disruption" of 1843, he remained as a minister of the Free

Church of Scotland. Among the most popular half dozen of his hymns is "I heard the voice of Jesus say," which he wrote at Kelso and included in his *Hymns Original and Selected,* 1846. Its title was "The Voice from Galilee." Doctor Macgill rendered it into Latin, his first line being, "Loquentem exaudivi."

TUNE: "Vox Dilecti" is the Latin for "Voice of the Beloved One," and as a tune title is derived from Doctor Bonar's hymn, "I heard the voice of Jesus," for which Dr. John B. Dykes composed this tune, while at Durham. (See No. 113.)

116. We Would See Jesus

TUNE: *"Cullingworth"*

ANNA B. WARNER   EDWIN MOSS

Anna B. Warner and her sister, Sarah Warner, daughters of Henry W. Warner, were both novelists; the former being author of *Say and Seal,* the latter of *Queechy.* In some of their literary work they collaborated as "the Wetherill Sisters." "Amy Lothrop" was the pseudonym of Anna Warner. Her hymn, "We would see Jesus," was included in her novel, *Dollars and Cents,* 1852, which the following year was republished in London, and was renamed *Speculation; or the Glen-Luna Family.* Miss Warner was a native of New York State.

TUNE: Edwin Moss, born in 1838, became a schoolmaster in Cardiff, Wales, at the age of twenty. Eight years later he came to London, where he made a success as a music teacher, and composed some hymn-tunes; among them "Cullingworth" and "Llandaff" being the best.

117. No, Not Despairingly

TUNE: *"Kedron"*

HORATIUS BONAR   MISS A. B. SPRATT

Doctor Bonar's "No, not despairingly," was written as a Lenten hymn and appeared first in his *Hymns of Faith and Hope,* Third Series, in 1866. Its title was "Confession and Peace." (See No. 115.)

TUNE: The tune, "Kedron," is attributed to Miss A. B. Spratt, of whom there is no information available.

118. Thou Hidden Love of God

TUNE: *"St. Petersburg"*

GERHARD TERSTEEGEN
Translated by JOHN WESLEY

DIMITRI BORTNIANSKY

Tersteegen has been regarded as one of the greatest three hymn-writers of the Reformed Church in Germany, though he early severed his connection with its services and devoted himself to the informal worship and practice of the Quietists. He became an influential teacher of mystical religion, and eventually gave up his work as a weaver of silk ribbons to devote his whole time to the translation of works upon this theme. His addresses were published in thirty-three volumes after his death. His hymns, mystical in tone and deeply spiritual, were many. One of them, which he wrote while in charge of the "Pilgerhutte" or spiritual retreat at Otterbeck in Germany, "Verborgne Gottesliebe du," was translated by John Wesley into the English lines, beginning, "Thou hidden love of God," in 1736, while Wesley was in Savannah, Georgia. (See No. 12.)

TUNE: Dimitri Stephanovitch Bortniansky (1751-1825), a Russian composer, who was chapelmaster to the Empress Catherine, composed the tune, "St. Petersburg," which during the Czaristic regime was immensely popular among Russian Christians.

119. Purer Yet and Purer

TUNE: *"Morley"*

ANONYMOUS

THOMAS MORLEY

Little is known of the origin of the hymn, "Purer Yet and Purer," save that it was first printed anonymously in this country in the *Sabbath Hymn Book,* 1858.

TUNE: Thomas Morley, composer of the tune which bears his name as its title, "Morley," was an English composer who was born in 1557 and died in 1603.

120. Break Thou the Bread of Life

TUNE: *"Bread of Life"*

MARY A. LATHBURY

WILLIAM F. SHERWIN

The Rev. Dr. John H. Vincent, afterwards bishop of the Methodist Episcopal Church, who was founder of the

Chautauqua Assembly on the shores of Lake Chautauqua, New York, eager to have a Bible study song for the normal classes in that institution, asked Miss Mary A. Lathbury to write such a hymn; and "Break Thou the bread of life" was the result, transforming Lake Chautauqua into the Sea of Galilee, and invoking the presence of the Master, as when he broke the bread to the multitudes. (See No. 30.)

TUNE: The melody, "Bread of Life," was composed in 1877 by another prominent Chautauquan, William Fiske Sherwin, a Baptist who had an important part in the early musical programs at Chautauqua, New York. It derives its title from Miss Lathbury's hymn, for which it was especially composed. (See No. 30.)

121. Nearer, My God, to Thee

TUNE: *"Bethany"*

SARAH F. ADAMS   LOWELL MASON

Sarah Flower, who in 1834 became Mrs. William B. Adams, was born in Harlow, Essex, England, 1805, and died in London, 1848. Her father, Benjamin Flower, was editor of the *Cambridge Intelligencer*. In 1841 she contributed thirteen hymns to *Hymns and Anthems,* edited by the Rev. W. J. Fox, her pastor in a London Unitarian Church, and among them was "Nearer, my God, to Thee" (No. 85 in that book), which describes Jacob's spiritual experience at Bethel, and has been adopted by millions of worshippers as their own prayer.

TUNE: Dr. Lowell Mason composed the tune, "Bethany," in 1856 to the hymn, "Nearer, my God, to Thee." (See No. 21.)

122. O Lord of Life and Love and Power

TUNE: *"Ellacombe"*

ELLA S. ARMITAGE   Gesang Buch der Herzogl

At Waterhead, Oldham, England, they were opening a new Sunday school in 1875 and Mrs. Ella S. Armitage was asked to write a hymn for that occasion. She was the wife of the Rev. E. Armitage, who was theological professor in the Congregational United College at Bradford. She consented to write it, and the result was the hymn, "O Lord of life and love and power," which was afterwards published in *The Garden of the Lord,* 1881.

TUNE: The hymn-tune, "Ellacombe," is anonymous: it was first found in a German hymnal, *Gesang Buch der Herzogl.*

123.   I Would Be True

TUNE: *"Peek"*

HOWARD ARNOLD WALTER   JOSEPH YATES PEEK

The Rev. Howard Arnold Walter, a native of New Britain, Connecticut, August 19, 1883, was graduated at Princeton University, 1905, and that year entered Hartford Theological Seminary. The next year, 1906-07, he taught English in Waseda University, Tokyo, Japan. Returning for the rest of his course, he was graduated in Hartford, 1909, and went to Edinburgh, Glasgow, and Göttingen to study and work in the institutional churches of those cities. In 1910 he married Miss Marguerite B. Darlington of Brooklyn, New York, and became assistant pastor of the Asylum Hill Congregational Church, Hartford. In 1913 John R. Mott invited him to become Literary Secretary to Mohammedan Students for the Y. M. C. A. of India and Ceylon. He had a weak heart and the doctors told him he would live but five years if he went to India. But his creed, as expressed in his hymn, "I would be true," contained the couplet,

> I would be strong, for there is much to suffer;
> I would be brave, for there is much to dare.

Knowing his weakness, he went to Lahore, wrought a remarkable work among the students there, and lived a Christian life that was a real inspiration to hundreds. His sudden death on November 1, 1918, proved the doctors to be right, and crowned with sacrifice a wonderful life of service. His hymn is inscribed on a memorial tablet, which was unveiled in his home church, The First Church of Christ, New Britain, on February 14, 1926.

TUNE: The tune, "Peek," composed for these words, takes its title from the last name of its composer, Joseph Yates Peek, a contemporary English musician.

124. Keep Thyself Pure! Christ's Soldier, Hear
Tune: *"Melrose"*

Adelaide M. Plumptre   Frederick C. Maker

Adelaide M. Plumptre wrote "Keep thyself pure! Christ's soldier, hear." No information about her has been disclosed.

TUNE: Frederick Charles Maker, born in 1844, was an English composer of church music. He wrote many anthems and hymn-tunes, among the latter being "Melrose."

125. As Pants the Hart for Cooling Streams
Tune: *"Simpson"*

Tate and Brady   From "The Crucifixion" by Louis Spohr
Altered by Henry F. Lyte

In an age when in England only metrical psalms were countenanced for public use in church worship, dissatisfactions with the prevailing version of the psalms (known as "Sternhold and Hopkins") led to the new version, developed by Nahum Tate and Nicholas Brady, and known as the Tate and Brady Psalter, which against conservative opposition finally supplanted the older version. "As pants the hart for cooling streams," our surviving reminder in common use of that psalter, was one of the "few examples of sweet and simple verse" which it contained. It is a translation of Psalm 42. The Rev. Henry F. Lyte, author of "Abide with me," rewrote the third stanza in the form in which we now use it. (See No. 208.)

TUNE: Louis Spohr, famous German violinist and composer (1784-1859), wrote many operas, symphonies, and oratorios from one of which was taken our melody, "Simpson."

126. My Faith Looks Up to Thee
Tune: *"Olivet"*

Ray Palmer   Lowell Mason

Before entering the ministry, but immediately following his graduation from Yale College, Ray Palmer (1808-1887) taught school near St. Paul's Church, Fulton Street,

New York city. While recovering from an illness, he wrote his now famous hymn, "My faith looks up to Thee" (he was then not quite twenty-three years old). Concerning its composition he later said:

I gave form to what I felt, by writing, with little effort, the stanzas. I recollect I wrote them with very tender emotion and ended the last line with tears. I composed them with a deep consciousness of my own needs, without the slightest thought of writing for another eye, and least of all of writing a hymn for Christian worship.

TUNE: Two years after Ray Palmer wrote "My faith looks up to Thee," it was placed in the hands of Lowell Mason by his colleague, Thomas Hastings, with whom he was then preparing a new hymnal, *Spiritual Hymns for Social Worship,* 1832. Mason liked the hymn so well that he composed the tune, "Olivet," for it, and together they appeared in this hymnal. (See No. 21.)

127. O Jesus, I Have Promised
TUNE: *"Angel's Story"*

JOHN E. BODE   ARTHUR H. MANN

The Rev. John E. Bode, a graduate of Eton and Oxford, was rector of the Church of England at Westwall, Oxfordshire, and at Castle Camps, Cambridgeshire; and for a while a tutor and classical examiner in Christ Church, Oxford. He wrote his famous hymn, "O Jesus, I have promised," for confirmation services of his two sons and his daughter, and it appeared in the appendix of *Psalms and Hymns,* published in 1869 by the Society for the Propagation of Christian Knowledge. Sometimes it is printed thus, "O Jesus, we have promised."

TUNE: "Angel's Story" was composed by Dr. Arthur Henry Mann for Emily Huntington Miller's hymn, "I love to hear the story, which angel voices tell," and derives its title from that hymn. It was printed first in the *Methodist Sunday School Tune Book,* London, 1881. Doctor Mann, a native of Norwich, England, May 16, 1850, was an Oxonian, '74, and received from Oxford his degree of Doctor of Music in 1882. He became chorister in Norwich Cathedral and later organist in King's College, Cambridge. As hymn-book editor and composer of many hymn-tunes, he has become famous in church music.

128. Jesus, Thy Boundless Love to Me

Tune: *"St. Catherine"*

Paul Gerhardt
Translated by John Wesley

James G. Walton

"Jesu Christ, mein schönstes Licht" was the first line of a hymn by Paul Gerhardt (1607-1676), which John Wesley found in the Herrnhut *Gesang Buch* of the Moravians and translated into our English hymn, "Jesus, Thy boundless love to me." In 1655 Gerhardt married the daughter of Andreas Barthold, in whose family at Berlin he was tutor for some years, while occasionally preaching in that city. Later, he gave his whole time to preaching and pastoral work at Mittenwalde and then in Berlin. Political entanglements led to his being deposed and he suffered many hardships. His wife and four of his five children died. But to the end he remained strong in his faith and sweet in his spirit. (See Nos. 53 and 12.)

TUNE: James G. Walton, writer of the hymn-tune, "St. Catherine," was an English composer, born in 1821.

129. Take My Life, and Let It Be

Tune: *"Ellingham"*

Frances R. Havergal

Nathaniel S. Godfrey

In the Havergal Manuscripts is to be found the following account, which Miss Frances Ridley Havergal gave of the origin of her hymn, "Take my life, and let it be":

Perhaps you will be interested to know the origin of the consecration hymn, "Take my life." I went for a little visit of five days (to Areley House). There were ten persons in the house, some unconverted and long prayed for, some converted, but not rejoicing Christians. He gave me the prayer, "Lord, give me *all* in this house!" And He just *did*. Before I left the house every one had got a blessing. The last night of my visit after I had retired, the governess asked me to go to the two daughters. They were crying, &c.; then and there both of them trusted and rejoiced; it was nearly midnight. I was too happy to sleep, and passed most of the night in praise and renewal of my own consecration; and these little couplets formed themselves, and chimed in my heart one after another till they finished with *"Ever, Only, ALL for Thee!"*

(See No. 110.)

TUNE: "Ellingham" was composed by Nathaniel S. Godfrey, an unknown composer.

70

130. Love Divine, All Loves Excelling

TUNE: *"Beecher"*

CHARLES WESLEY

JOHN ZUNDEL

In *Hymns for Those that Seek and Those that have Redemption in the Blood of Jesus Christ,* published by John Wesley in 1747, appeared for the first time the hymn by his brother, Charles, "Love divine, all loves excelling." The line, "Take away our power of sinning," was altered to "bent to sinning" by Bishops Coke and Asbury when they prepared the first hymnal of the Methodist Episcopal Church in America, as being a truer theological expression. (See No. 100.)

TUNE: John Zundel, born December 10, 1815, in Germany, after being bandmaster and organist in St. Petersburg, came to this country in 1847. During the next twenty years he was three times organist of Plymouth Church, Brooklyn, New York, under the pastorate of the Rev. Dr. Henry Ward Beecher. Hence the title of the tune. He edited *Psalmody,* 1855, in which ninety-seven of his own tunes were included, and some of these appeared in the *Plymouth Collection,* edited by Beecher, the same year. He died in Germany, 1882.

131. Blest Are the Pure in Heart

TUNE: *"Greenwood"*

JOHN KEBLE

JOSEPH E. SWEETSER

The Rev. John Keble wrote his hymn, "Blest are the pure in heart," on October 10, 1819, while he was college tutor at Oriel. It was published in his famous book of devotional poetry, *The Christian Year,* 1827. The year before its publication he was curate of Hursley, to which church he returned in 1836 as vicar, having been professor of Poetry at Oxford for some part of the interim. His poetry and his preaching both did much to revive the spiritual life of the Church of England in his day. (See No. 25.)

TUNE: Joseph E. Sweetser, composer of the hymn-tune, "Greenwood," was an Englishman, who was born in 1825 and died in 1873. He became well known as a composer of vocal music.

132. Forever Here My Rest Shall Be

TUNE: *"Avon"*

CHARLES WESLEY   HUGH WILSON

"Christ Our Righteousness" was the title of Charles Wesley's hymn, "Forever here my rest shall be," as it appeared in his *Hymns and Sacred Poems,* 1740. It is based on 1 Corinthians 1, 30. (See No. 100.)

TUNE: The original title of the tune, "Avon," was "Fenwick," named for the town in Ayrshire, Scotland, where its composer, Hugh Wilson, was born, 1764. It was first published on sheets, about 1802. But somewhat altered, it found its first hymnal publication in *The Seraph,* edited by John Robertson, 1827. Wilson became a teacher of music and mathematics, a choir leader and a maker of sun-dials. In 1800 he settled in Pollokshaws, where he helped establish the first Sunday school. He died in 1824.

133. Oh! Still in Accents Sweet and Strong

TUNE: *"St. Mark"*

SAMUEL LONGFELLOW   HENRY J. GAUNTLETT

The Rev. Samuel Longfellow (1819-1892), graduate of Harvard, and Unitarian minister, was the brother of the celebrated American poet, Henry Wadsworth Longfellow. He served as pastor in Fall River, Massachusetts, Brooklyn, New York, and Germantown, Pennsylvania. He was editor, along with the Rev. S. Johnson, of the Unitarian collection, *Hymns of the Spirit,* which was published in 1864. And from this book has been taken his hymn, "Oh! still in accents sweet and strong," which was written as a missionary hymn.

TUNE: "St. Mark" is one of the best tunes composed by Dr. Henry J. Gauntlett (1806-1876), who was one of the musical pioneers of modern psalmody. An organist of fine ability and an editor of high standards, he was associated with the making of nearly every important English hymn-book from 1846 until his death in 1876.

134. Walk in the Light!

Tune: *"Manoah"*

Bernard Barton

Francis J. Haydn

The "Quaker Poet," Bernard Barton (1784-1849), began his career as apprentice to a shop-keeper in Halsted, Essex, England; later joined his brother in the coal and corn trade; acted as tutor in Liverpool; and for the last forty years of his life was a banker. With all his varied responsibilities, he found time and inspiration to compose a number of books of poems, including many hymns. "Walk in the light!" is one of twenty from his pen that are still in common use.

Tune: "Manoah" (See Nos. 87 and 17).

135. It May Not Be Our Lot to Wield

Tune: *"Abends"*

John G. Whittier

Herbert S. Oakeley

The fourth stanza of Whittier's poem, "Seedtime and Harvest," begins with the line, "It may not be our lot to wield." It was written about 1850, and was published in his *Miscellaneous Poems.* (See No. 2.)

TUNE: Sir Herbert Oakeley (1830-1905), composer of the tune, "Abends," was graduated from Rugby and Oxford University, and studied piano and organ in Germany. The University of Edinburgh made him a professor in 1865. He became distinguished as a composer of many vocal and instrumental pieces.

136. A Charge to Keep I Have

Tune: *"Boylston"*

Charles Wesley

Lowell Mason

"Keep the charge of the Lord, that ye die not" (Leviticus 8, 35) is the text on which Charles Wesley founded his hymn, "A charge to keep I have." In 1762 he published it in his *Short Scriptural Hymns.* (See No. 100.)

TUNE: The tune, "Boylston," named for a Massachusetts town, was composed by Lowell Mason in 1838, and appeared in *The Choir,* that same year. (See No. 21.)

137. Hark! the Voice of Jesus Calling

TUNE: *"Ellesdie"*

DANIEL MARCH   JOHANN C. W. A. MOZART

The Rev. Dr. Daniel March, an American Congregational minister, author of *Night Scenes in the Bible,* has told the following story about the writing of his hymn, "Hark! the voice of Jesus calling":

It was written at the impulse of the moment to follow a sermon I was to preach in Clinton St. Church to the Philadelphia Christian Association on the text, *Is. 6, 8.* That was some time in 1868.

Tune: Johann C. Wolfgang Adameus Mozart (1756-1791) achieved, through his orchestral works chiefly, the distinction of being one of the greatest composers in the history of music; although he died at the age of thirty-five. From his music is taken our hymn-tune, "Ellesdie."

138. Lead On, O King Eternal

TUNE: *"Lancashire"*

ERNEST W. SHURTLEFF   HENRY SMART

When the Rev. Ernest Warburton Shurtleff, afterwards a Congregational minister in Palmer and Plymouth, Massachusetts, and Minneapolis, Minnesota, was about to be graduated from the Andover Theological Seminary, 1887 (having previously been graduated from Harvard University), he wrote for his classmates as a parting hymn the lines, "Lead on, O King Eternal," and it was published that same year in *Hymns of the Faith.* Anyone reading through the hymn may readily sense its spirit of hope and courage, its fitness as a hymn of challenge for those young men about to enter the ministry.

TUNE: The tune, "Lancashire," which is now almost exclusively used for "Lead on, O King Eternal," in this country, was originally composed for Bishop Heber's hymn, "From Greenland's icy mountains," by the blind organist, Henry Smart, in 1836, to be sung at a missionary meeting in Blackburn, England. The tune was first published in *Psalms and Hymns for Divine Worship,* 1867, though not until a quarter of a century later to these words of Ernest W. Shurtleff. (See No. 7.)

139.   Awake, My Soul, Stretch Every Nerve
TUNE: *"Christmas"*

PHILIP DODDRIDGE   GEORGE F. HANDEL

Under the title, "Pressing on in the Christian Race," Doddridge's hymn, "Awake, my soul, stretch every nerve," was published by J. Orton in the posthumous collection of Doddridge's *Hymns*. In some subsequent hymnals the first line is given thus: "Awake, our souls, awake from sloth." The Rev. R. Bingham rendered it into Latin with this first line, "Sursum, mens mea! Strenue." (See No. 94.)

TUNE: The tune, "Christmas," was derived from the "Non vi piacque" in the opera, "Ciroë" (or "Cyrus"), 1728, by George Frederick Handel (1685-1759). Handel was born in Halle, Germany, the son of a surgeon. Much of his life was spent at Hanover as court musician, but he had great success in England, where his oratorios, especially the "Messiah," made him a great favorite.

140.   Am I a Soldier of the Cross
TUNE: *"Arlington"*

ISAAC WATTS   THOMAS A. ARNE

Isaac Watts's hymn, "Am I a soldier of the cross," appeared in the three-volume edition of his *Sermons,* published in 1721-1724, and was used to illustrate his sermon in the third volume on 1 Corinthians 16, 13. It was entitled "Holy Fortitude." (See No. 174.)

TUNE: The hymn-tune, "Arlington," or "Artaxerxes" (as it is sometimes called), was taken from a minuet in the overture to Thomas A. Arne's opera, "Artaxerxes," 1762. Ralph Harrison arranged it as a hymn-tune and published it in his hymnal, *Sacred Harmony*, 1784. Arne (1710-1778) received from Oxford the degree of Doctor of Music, 1759, in recognition of his pre-eminence as a composer of operas, a leader of bands at Drury Lane and Convent Garden, London, and as a teacher of music.

141.   The Son of God Goes Forth to War
TUNE: *"All Saints"*

REGINALD HEBER   HENRY S. CUTLER

Bishop Reginald Heber of the Church of England, missionary to Calcutta, India (where he died), wrote his hymn, "The Son of God goes forth to war," for St. Stephen's Day. The second stanza contains a reference to the martyred Stephen's vision of Christ, as he was being stoned to death:

> The martyr first, whose eagle eye
> Could pierce beyond the grave, *et seq.*

This hymn, like most of Heber's other hymns of fine literary flavor, was published by his widow in the posthumous collection, *Hymns Written and Adapted to the Weekly Church Services of the Year,* 1827. (See No. 27.)

TUNE: . Henry Stephen Cutler, composer of the hymn-tune, "All Saints," was born in Boston, 1825, and died in that city, 1902. He studied music in Germany, and on his return became organist of churches, successively, in Boston (Church of the Advent), New York (Trinity), Brooklyn, Providence, Philadelphia and Troy. His tune, "All Saints," has attained great popularity.

142.   Lord, Speak to Me That I May Speak

TUNE: *"Canonbury"*

FRANCES R. HAVERGAL   ROBERT A. SCHUMANN

Miss Havergal's hymn, "Lord, speak to me," was written on April 28, 1872, at Winterdyne, England, for the use of lay helpers in the church, and was entitled, "A Worker's Prayer." The text of the hymn is Romans 14, 7. That same year it was printed as one of Parlane's musical leaflets, and in 1874 was contained in Miss Havergal's *Under the Surface.* (See No. 110.)

TUNE: "Canonbury" (See No. 19).

143.   Fight the Good Fight

TUNE: *"Pentecost"*

JOHN S. B. MONSELL   WILLIAM BOYD

The Rev. Dr. John Samuel Bewley Monsell, a clergyman of the Church of England, published eleven volumes of poems. The fifth of these, *Hymns of Love and Praise for the Church's Year,* was published in 1863, twelve years before his tragic death, and contained his hymn on the

"Fight of Faith," "Fight the good fight with all thy might." (See No. 22.)

TUNE: The Rev. William Boyd, who composed the tune, "Pentecost," was a native of Jamaica, West Indies, 1840. The tune, published in *Thirty-two Hymn Tunes*, 1868, by Oxford composers, was set first to "Come, Holy Ghost, our hearts inspire," at the request of the Rev. S. Baring-Gould. The composer has said of it: "I walked, talked, slept, and ate with the words, and at last evolved the tune which I naturally named 'Pentecost.'" The composer died in 1927.

144. Onward, Christian Soldiers!

TUNE: *"St. Gertrude"*

SABINE BARING-GOULD   ARTHUR S. SULLIVAN

The Rev. Sabine Baring-Gould once wrote the following account of his hymn, "Onward, Christian soldiers!":

Whitmonday is a great day for school festivals in Yorkshire. One Whitmonday, thirty years ago (1865), it was arranged that our school should join forces with a neighboring village. I wanted the children to sing, when marching from one village to another, but couldn't think of anything quite suitable; so I sat up at night, resolved that I would write something myself. "Onward, Christian soldiers," was the result. It was written in great haste, and I am afraid some of the rhymes are faulty. Certainly nothing has surprised me more than its popularity. (See No. 28.)

TUNE: Sir Arthur S. Sullivan in the title of his tune, "St. Gertrude," has canonized his friend, Mrs. Gertrude Clay-Ker-Seymer, sister-in-law of Frederick Clay; for it was in her home in Hanford, Dorsetshire, where he often visited, that he wrote this tune to be sung first in their chapel with Sir Arthur at the little organ. First published in *The Musical Times,* December, 1871, it made its first hymnal appearance in *The Church Hymnary,* 1872. (See No. 73.)

145. The World's Astir! the Clouds of Storm

TUNE: *"Materna"*

FRANK MASON NORTH   SAMUEL A. WARD

The hymn, "The world's astir!" was written by the Rev. Dr. Frank Mason North in response to a request made by Dr. Abram W. Harris, then secretary of the

Methodist Episcopal Board of Education, for a hymn of inspiration for Children's Day to be used in the educational program for that occasion throughout the church. Doctor North was born in New York city, 1850, was graduated from Wesleyan University, 1872, from which institution he has received the degrees of A.B., A.M., D.D., and LL.D. He served many Methodist Episcopal pastorates in the New York and New York East Conferences; for twenty years was the executive officer of the New York City Missionary and Church Extension Society; and for twelve years the corresponding secretary of the Board of Foreign Missions, of which he is still the council secretary. He was president of the Federal Council of Churches of Christ in America, 1912-1916. He is author of many excellent hymns.

TUNE: Samuel A. Ward, the American composer, who wrote the tune, "Materna," was born in Newark, New Jersey, 1848, and died there in 1903. He was conductor of the Orpheus Club in Newark, and managed a piano and music establishment. The tune derives its name from the hymn to which it was first sung, "O mother dear, Jerusalem"; as "Materna" is the Latin for "mother."

146. Soldiers of the Cross, Arise!

TUNE: *"Caledonia"*

JARED B. WATERBURY   Scotch Tune

The Rev. Dr. Jared Bell Waterbury, born in New York city, August 11, 1799, was after his graduation from Yale College and Princeton Theological Seminary a Congregational clergyman, serving a number of pastorates in the east. He died in Brooklyn, December 31, 1876. When his friend, Joshua Leavitt, was preparing in 1830 the first volume of his tune book, *The Christian Lyre,* Waterbury contributed seven hymns, among them being "Soldiers of the cross, arise!" Each was headed, "Written for the Lyre," and signed "J. B. W."

TUNE: The old Scotch tune, "Caledonia," originally written in the scale of the bag-pipes, has led many an army on their march into battle, singing, "Scots wha hae wi' Wallace bled."

147. O Ye Who Dare Go Forth With God

TUNE: *"Land of Rest"*

W. RUSSELL BOWIE

RICHARD S. NEWMAN

The Rev. Dr. Walter Russell Bowie was born in Richmond, Virginia, October 8, 1882, and was graduated from Harvard, 1904. Entering the ministry of the Protestant Episcopal Church, he has served many churches as rector, the last two being St. Paul's, Richmond, and Grace Church, New York city, where he is now in charge. He is author of nine books and was editor of the *Southern Churchman*. His hymns (and he has written many) are filled with the Christian spirit of social service and brotherhood, and are among the best America has produced. "O ye who dare go forth with God" is a startling challenge to service.

TUNE: Richard Newman was a local musical manager in Boston, Massachusetts. It is not certain that he was the composer of "Land of Rest."

148. Stand Up, Stand Up for Jesus

TUNE: *"Webb"*

GEORGE DUFFIELD

GEORGE J. WEBB

The Rev. Dr. George Duffield, Junior, in *Lyra Sacra Americana* tells this story of the origin of his hymn, "Stand up, stand up for Jesus":

I caught its inspiration from the dying words of that noble young clergyman, Rev. Dudley Atkins Tyng, rector of the Epiphany Church, Philadelphia, who died about 1854 *(should be 1858)*. His last words were, "Tell them to stand up for Jesus; now let us sing a hymn." As he had been much persecuted in those pre-slavery days for his persistent course in pleading the cause of the oppressed, it was thought that these words had a peculiar significance in his mind; as if he had said, "Stand up for Jesus in the person of the down-trodden slave." (Luke 5, 18.)

TUNE: George James Webb was an English organist and voice teacher, a native of Salisbury, 1803. He came to this country in his twenties and established himself in Boston, was for a time conductor of the Musical Fund Society. In 1870 he went to Orange, New Jersey, to teach, and lived here until his death, 1887. Once while crossing the Atlantic Ocean, he composed a tune to the words, " 'Tis dawn, the lark is singing," which became a popular song. This, adapted to Duffield's hymn, "Stand up, stand up for Jesus," became our hymn-tune, "Webb," so named for its composer.

149. Faith of Our Fathers!

TUNE: *"St. Catherine"*

FREDERICK W. FABER   JAMES G. WALTON

Father Faber, a priest of the Roman Catholic Church, but formerly of the Church of England, wrote two hymns, beginning "Faith of our fathers!"—one for England and one for Ireland, which were published in his *Jesus and Mary: or Catholic Hymns for Singing and Reading,* 1849. The third line of our hymn was originally written thus, "How Ireland's heart beats high with joy." The hymn has been altered to suit Protestant needs. (See No. 38.)

TUNE: "St. Catherine" (See No. 128).

150. Teach Me, My God and King

TUNE: *"Mornington"*

GEORGE HERBERT. Altered   THE EARL OF MORNINGTON

The Rev. George Herbert's hymn, "Teach me, my God and king," was altered to its present lines by John Wesley. In its original form, as it appeared in *The Temple,* 1633, one may find the lines which explain its title, "The Elixir." Published by Nicholas Ferrar, his literary executor, in the year following his death, *The Temple* attained great popularity and the thirteenth edition was printed in 1709. William T. Brooke has said: "It is meditative rather than hymnic in character, and was never intended for use in public worship." Nevertheless, this hymn with its simple, quaint expressions has proved to be of great value in worship services.

Tune: "Mornington" (See No. 12).

151. Work for the Night Is Coming

TUNE: *"Work Song"*

ANNIE L. COGHILL   LOWELL MASON

Miss Annie Louisa Walker, who was born in Staffordshire, England, 1836, married Harry Coghill in 1884.

When she moved to Canada many of her poetic compositions began to appear in Canadian newspapers, among them in 1854 being the song, "Work for the night is coming." It is sometimes confused with another hymn, having the same first line, written in the same year (1854) by Sidney Dyer for a Sunday school in Indianapolis. Her hymn was afterwards published in Miss Walker's collection of hymns and poems, *Leaves from the Backwoods.*

TUNE: Lowell Mason composed his tune, "Work Song," especially for Mrs. Coghill's hymn. (See No. 21.)

152. There's a Light Upon the Mountains

TUNE: *"Mt. Holyoke"*
HENRY BURTON   M. L. WOSTENHOLM

The Rev. Dr. Henry Burton, a clergyman of the Wesleyan Methodist Church in England, died in West Kirby, England, in April, 1930, after serving in many pastorates in his native country. He was educated in Beloit College and spent some years of his young manhood in this country. His hymn, "There's a light upon the mountains," written in his later years, is full of the faith and optimism of Christian youth, confident that a better day is about to dawn.

TUNE: A recent English composer, M. L. Wostenholm, has caught in his tune, "Mt. Holyoke," the optimistic spirit of Doctor Burton's great hymn, "There's a light upon the mountains."

153. Where Cross the Crowded Ways of Life

TUNE: *"Germany"*
FRANK MASON NORTH   LUDWIG VAN BEETHOVEN

The Rev. Dr. Frank Mason North was editor of a monthly magazine, *The Christian City,* published in connection with the work of the New York City Missionary and Church Extension Society of the Methodist Episcopal Church, of which he was for many years the executive secretary. In this magazine, 1903, first appeared his hymn, "Where cross the crowded ways of life." He wrote it at the request of Professor Caleb T. Winchester of Wesleyan University for *The Methodist Hymnal* of 1905. It has since become the most widely published of the standard hymns written in this century. It was based on Matthew 22, 9, on which text Doctor North was preparing a sermon at the time the hymn was composed. (See No. 145.)

TUNE: The tune, here entitled "Germany," appeared in William Gardiner's *Sacred Melodies* as taken from Beethoven. (See No. 37.) Grove's *Dictionary,* however, questions this source.

154. Oft in Danger, Oft in Woe

TUNE: *"University College"*

HENRY KIRKE WHITE   HENRY J. GAUNTLETT

The author of the hymn, "Oft in danger," in its original form, Henry Kirke White, died when he was twenty-one years old; but he had already written a group of poems of such excellence as to attract the favorable attention of the whole English literary world. Southey published his literary *Remains,* prefaced with high praise for his art. He was converted from irreligion during his college days through reading Scott's *Force of Truth* and through conversations with his friend, R. W. Almond (who later became rector of St. Peter's, Nottingham, England). After White's death in 1806 they found among his mathematical papers the hymn, "Much in sorrow, oft in woe." A fourteen-year-old girl, Frances Sara Fuller-Maitland (born three years after White's death), revised this hymn in its present form.

TUNE: The tune, "University College," was first published in *Church Hymn- and Tune-Book,* 1846, edited by Henry J. Gauntlett, the English composer who wrote this tune. This book signalized a new era in psalmody, wherein it set the style for the "fixed tune principle" in England. (See No. 133.)

155. Once to Every Man and Nation

TUNE: *"Austria"*

JAMES RUSSELL LOWELL   FRANCIS J. HAYDN

The American poet, James Russell Lowell, in December, 1845, wrote a poem, "The Present Crisis," against the war with Mexico, in which he argued that annexation to the United States of any considerable portion of Mexico would only add to the American territory in which slavery was permitted. The first line of the poem was, "When a deed is done for freedom." It was published in Lowell's *Poems,* Volume 2, 1849. From this poem a cento was taken which forms our own stirring hymn of social justice, "Once to every man and nation."

TUNE: "Austria" (See Nos. 90 and 17).

156. When Wilt Thou Save the People

TUNE: *"Commonwealth"*

EBENEZER ELLIOTT   JOSIAH BOOTH

One of the earliest English hymns of social justice was Ebenezer Elliott's "When wilt Thou save the people." He was known as "the Corn Law Rhymer," for his many poems on the rights of man, which during the great social excitement over the Corn Laws in England proved to be very popular. They were published chiefly in a newspaper at Sheffield, where he spent most of his life. Born at Rotherham, Yorkshire, in 1781, he died at Barnsley, Yorkshire, in 1849.

TUNE: Josiah Booth, an English organist, born in 1852, composed the tune, "Commonwealth," to Ebenezer Elliott's hymn, "When wilt Thou save the people"; setting the challenge of the first quatrain in minor, and the pleading prayer of the second quatrain in the major mode.

157. Love Thyself Last

TUNE: *"Lanherne"*

ANONYMOUS   HENRY HAYMAN

"Love thyself last" is anonymous. It serves well to express the true spirit of Christian service, a whole-hearted, glad unselfishness; and the hymn is coming into increasing favor.

TUNE: Sir Henry Heyman, born in Oakland, California, knighted by King Kalakua of Hawaii, was the dean of San Francisco violinists. It is not certain that he was the composer of "Lanherne."

158.   O Master, Let Me Walk With Thee

TUNE: *"Maryton"*

WASHINGTON GLADDEN   H. PERCY SMITH

The Rev. Dr. Washington Gladden, one of the foremost leaders of the Congregational Church in America, was born in Pottsgrove, Pennsylvania, 1836, and was graduated from Williams College. He served as pastor of a number of Congregational churches and was editor of the *Independent* and of *Sunday Afternoon*. In the latter periodical was first published his hymn of Christian service, "O Master, let me walk with Thee," on the theme, "Walking with God."

TUNE: The Rev. Henry Percy Smith, composer of the hymn-tune, "Maryton," was born in England, 1825, entered the ministry of the Church of England, and died in 1898.

159.   We Knelt Before Kings

TUNE: *"Hanover"*

WILLIAM P. MERRILL   WILLIAM CROFT

The Rev. Dr. William P. Merrill, pastor of the Brick Presbyterian Church, is the author of a number of hymns, stressing the social emphasis which is finding wide expression in the twentieth century. On reading Lloyd George's famous speech in the English Parliament on the proposed 1909 budget, which provided for the social needs of the people, as had no previous budget, he was stirred to write his hymn, "We knelt before kings, we bent before lords." It was published in the *Continent*, 1913. (See No. 280.)

TUNE: "Hanover" was composed by Dr. William Croft, for years organist in the Royal Chapel of the House of Hanover. (See No. 91.) It was first published in John Playford's *Supplement to the New Version of the Psalms,* 1708.

160.   Master, No Offering
TUNE: *"Love's Offering"*
EDWIN P. PARKER

EDWIN P. PARKER

In January, 1860, the Rev. Dr. Edwin Pond Parker became pastor of the Second Church of Christ in Hartford, Connecticut, and while serving there he edited a number of hymnals, such as *The Book of Praise* and *The Christian Hymnal,* and also wrote many hymns, the most popular of which is "Master, no offering costly and sweet." He penned it in 1888 to use it at the close of a sermon he was about to preach in his Hartford pulpit, and published it the next year in his *Christian Hymnal.*

TUNE: "Love's Offering" was composed especially for the hymn, "Master, no offering," by the author of the words, Doctor Parker, in one of the rare instances of music and words being both written by the same person, and continuing together in common use.

161.   Rise Up, O Men of God
TUNE: *"Oxnam"*
WILLIAM P. MERRILL

ROBERT G. McCUTCHAN

When the Men and Religion Movement, which was sweeping through American Protestantism, came to New York city, the Rev. Dr. William P. Merrill was stirred to write this hymn, "Rise up, O men of God." (See No. 280.)

TUNE: The tune, "Oxnam," by Dean Robert G. McCutchan of DePauw University, was named for President Oxnam of that University in Greencastle, Indiana, who had recently assumed his new duties as president, when the tune was composed. (See No. 105.)

162. God's Trumpet Wakes the Slumbering World
TUNE: *"Christmas"*
SAMUEL LONGFELLOW

GEORGE F. HANDEL

The "Call to Duty," beginning, "God's trumpet wakes the slumbering world," first appeared anonymously in Johnson's *Hymns of the Spirit,* 1864. But after the death of the Rev. Samuel Longfellow on October 3, 1892, his niece, Miss Alice Longfellow, published his hymns in a book, entitled *Hymns and Verses,* and his authorship of this hymn is here established. (See No. 133.)

TUNE: "Christmas" (See No. 139).

163. My Master Was a Worker

TUNE: *"Seasons"*

WILLIAM GEORGE TARRANT   Arranged from MENDELSSOHN

The Rev. William George Tarrant was born in England in 1853, and became a Unitarian minister. He was editor of *The Inquirer* while pastor of the Wandsworth Unitarian Christian Church. He also edited the *Essex Hall Hymnal* in 1890.. The best known of his hymns is "My Master was a worker."

TUNE: The tune, "Seasons," was taken from the melody of a glee by Felix Mendelssohn Bartholdy (1809-1847), the famous German composer. In many fields of composition he achieved greatness; overtures, symphonies, piano works and oratorios ("St. Paul," "Hymn of Praise," and "Elijah").

164. O Brother Man, Fold to Thy Heart

TUNE: *"Strength and Stay"*

JOHN G. WHITTIER   JOHN B. DYKES

John G. Whittier's poem, "Worship," which he wrote in 1848 and published in his *Poems* in 1850, contains the lines which comprise our hymn, "O brother man, fold to thy heart thy brother." (See No. 2.)

TUNE: "Strength and Stay," the hymn-tune by the Rev. John B. Dykes (See No. 113), is better known in England than in this country. He composed it in 1875.

165. Thou Lord of Life, Our Saving Health

TUNE: *"Grace Church"*

SAMUEL LONGFELLOW   IGNACE PLEYEL

"Thou Lord of life, our saving health" was composed by the Rev. Samuel Longfellow in 1886, while he was pastor of the Unitarian Church in Germantown, Pennsylvania. It was written for use "In Sickness." (See No. 133.)

TUNE: Ignace Joseph Pleyel (1757-1831) was the composer of an instrumental melody, from which the hymn-tune, "Grace Church," has been arranged. He was born in Ruppersthal, Austria, the twenty-first son of his father. He enjoyed the rare advantage of studying under Haydn and developed into a prolific composer. He managed a music and piano house in Paris after the French Revolution. A number of hymn-tunes have been taken from his larger instrumental works. (See Nos. 174 and 258.)

166. Earth Is Waking, Day Is Breaking!

TUNE: *"Daybreak"*

ANONYMOUS   FELIX MENDELSSOHN-BARTHOLDY

"Earth is waking" is a joyous hymn of labor. Its authorship is unknown. Since its appearance in *Social Hymns,* 1914, it has been included in many American hymnals.

TUNE: The hymn-tune, "Daybreak," is a four-part arrangement of the aria, "If with all your hearts ye truly seek me," from Mendelssohn's oratorio, "Elijah." (See No. 163.)

167. The Bread That Giveth Strength

TUNE: *"Caroline"*

ANONYMOUS   ROBERT G. MCCUTCHAN

The authorship of "The bread that giveth strength" is unknown. It is an excellent hymn of aspiration for greater Christian service.

TUNE: The tune, "Caroline," by Dean Robert G. McCutchan, was named for his wife. (See No. 105.)

168. Jesus, Thou Divine Companion

TUNE: *"Love Divine"*

HENRY VAN DYKE   GEORGE F. LE JEUNE

"Jesus, Thou divine Companion" was written by the Rev. Dr. Henry van Dyke in 1909. Born in Germantown, Pennsylvania, 1852, Doctor van Dyke has had a distinguished career as a Presbyterian clergyman, his last pastorate being in the Brick Presbyterian Church, New York city, when he was made Moderator of the General Assembly of the Presbyterian Church; as a man of letters, author of many widely read volumes of prose and poetry; as professor of English Literature in Princeton University for twenty-three years; and as United States Minister to the Netherlands and Luxemburg, 1913-1917, including the first years of the World War.

TUNE: The tune, "Love Divine," was written by the English composer, George Fitz-Curwood Le Jeune (1842-1904), for Charles Wesley's hymn, "Love divine, all loves excelling," and derives its title from this hymn.

169.   O Holy City Seen of John
TUNE: *"Morwellham"*
W. RUSSELL BOWIE   CHARLES H. STEGGALL

The Rev. Dr. W. Russell Bowie wrote his stirring hymn, "O Holy City seen of John," in 1909, when he was rector of the Emmanuel Protestant Episcopal Church in Greenwood, Virginia. (See No. 147). It pictures the sordid social conditions which challenge Christians to bestir themselves in Christ's name and hasten the coming of the Kingdom of God upon earth.

TUNE: Dr. Charles H. Steggall, composer of the tune, "Morwellham," was born in London, England, 1826, was educated at the Royal Academy of Music, in which he was later professor, and made a great name as organist at Lincoln's, from 1864 until his death in 1905; as composer of many hymn-tunes; and as editor of *Church Psalmody*, 1849, and *Hymns for the Church of England*, 1865.

170.   Thy Kingdom Come, on Bended Knee
TUNE: *"Filius Dei"*
FREDERICK L. HOSMER   ALFRED R. GAUL

In 1891 the Rev. Frederick L. Hosmer, Unitarian pastor, then stationed at Cleveland, Ohio, wrote the hymn, "Thy kingdom come, on bended knee," for the commencement of the Meadville (Pennsylvania) Theological School which was held on June 12 of that year. It was published in *The Thought of God,* Second Series, 1894. Its title was "The Day of God," and it bore that legend,

"M. T. S., June 12, 1891," a reference to the Meadville commencement. (See No. 273).

TUNE: Alfred Robert Gaul, composer of "Filius Dei" (a Latin title, meaning "The Son of God," and referring to the hymn of that first line), was an English composer and organist. Born in Norwich, 1837, he died in Birmingham, 1913. He is best known in this country for his sacred cantatas, "The Holy City" and "Ruth," though he wrote other cantatas, part-songs and glees, and an oratorio, "Hezekiah."

171. These Things Shall Be: A Loftier Race

TUNE: "*Mozart*"

JOHN A. SYMONDS   Arranged from MOZART

The distinguished British scholar, John Addington Symonds, a graduate of Balliol College, Oxford, was famous for his *History of the Italian Renaissance* and other able studies, chiefly in the classical field. One of his many poems was the hymn, "These things shall be." It was taken from the fourth and subsequent stanzas of his poem, "A Vista," beginning with the line, "Sad heart, what will the future bring," which appeared in his book of poems, *New and Old,* 1880.

TUNE: The tune, "Mozart," is named for the great German composer, Johann C. W. A. Mozart, from whose work the melody was taken and arranged as a hymn-tune. (See No. 137.)

172. Must Jesus Bear the Cross Alone

TUNE: "*Maitland*"

THOMAS SHEPHERD. Altered   GEORGE N. ALLEN

At least the first stanza of the old hymn, "Must Jesus bear the cross alone," was written by the Rev. Thomas Shepherd (1665-1739), who left the ministry of the Church of England to become pastor of Castle Hill Meeting House, an Independent church in Nottingham, England. Years later, the Rev. Dr. Philip Doddridge served this church as minister. The first line of the original hymn was "Shall Simon bear Thy cross alone?" The hymn is found first in Shepherd's *Penitential Cries,* 1692.

Who wrote the other stanzas is a mystery. Some think the third stanza is by George N. Allen.

TUNE: George N. Allen, whether he amended the hymn or not, was composer of the tune, "Maitland." He edited *The Social and Sabbath Hymn Book,* in which the altered hymn and this tune appeared together in 1849.

173. In the Hour of Trial

TUNE: *"Penitence"*

JAMES MONTGOMERY. Altered by FRANCES A. HUTTON SPENCER LANE

James Montgomery (1771-1854) dated his original manuscript of "In the hour of trial" October 13, 1834. By that time he had retired from the editorship of *The Sheffield Iris,* and, the year before the hymn was written, he received an annual pension from the King of two hundred pounds. The original second line, "Jesus, pray for me," being challenged as to its theological implications, Montgomery changed it at Sheffield on April 25, 1835, to "Jesus, stand by me." Others afterwards altered it to "help Thou me," or "plead for me," which is our present accepted form. (See No. 51.)

TUNE: Spencer Lane, composer of the tune, "Penitence," was an American organist, born in 1843, who was also a manufacturer of musical instruments. He died in 1903.

174. My God, How Endless Is Thy Love

TUNE: *"St. Polycarp"*

ISAAC WATTS   IGNACE PLEYEL

"A Song for Morning or Evening" was the title which Doctor Watts gave to his hymn, "My God, how endless is Thy love," as it was published in his *Hymns and Spiritual Songs,* 1709. The Rev. Dr. Isaac Watts (1674-1748) has been somewhat inaccurately called "the Father of the English hymn." But there were many good English hymns written before his day; though "man-made" hymns were not allowed to be sung in the churches of England, owing to the peculiar veneration for metrical psalms, as translations of the Word of God. Watts liberated English worship from this superstition, rewrote the "Psalms of David," as they were then known, in New Testament language; and added many evangelical hymns, which found favor among the Non-conformist churches almost universally. Born at Southampton, he was the son of a defiant Non-conformist, who suffered imprisonment for his convictions. Watts went to a Dissenting Academy; and later entered the Christian ministry, serving an Independent Church in Mark Lane. His *Horae Lyricae* was published in 1705; his *Hymns and Spiritual Songs,* 1707; *Psalms,* 1719, and *Divine Songs for Children,* 1720. For thirty-six years he lived in the home of Sir Thomas Abney, in Herts., and for the last thirteen years in Stoke Newington. His fifty-two publications exerted a dominating influence over English hymnody.

TUNE: The tune, "St. Polycarp," is taken from a melody by the Austrian composer, Ignace Pleyel. (See No. 165.)

175. If on a Quiet Sea

TUNE: *"Selvin"*

AUGUSTUS M. TOPLADY. Altered   Arranged by LOWELL MASON

The Rev. Augustus M. Toplady's hymn, "Your harps, ye trembling saints," was first printed in the *Gospel Magazine,* February, 1772, under the title, "Weak Believers Encouraged." Its first hymnal appearance was in Toplady's *Hymns on Sacred Subjects,* 1856. From this hymn was taken a cento, beginning "If through unruffled seas," published in *Songs for the Sanctuary* in this country, 1865; or "If on a quiet sea," as we have it in its present form. It is doubtful, however, if Toplady wrote the first stanza of this cento. (See No. 104.)

TUNE: "Selvin" was one of many melodies which Lowell Mason arranged and adapted as hymn-tunes. (See No. 21.)

176. This Is My Father's World

TUNE: *"Terra Beata"*

MALTBIE D. BABCOCK

Traditional English Melody
Arranged by S. F. L.

The Rev. Dr. Maltbie D. Babcock's hymn, "This is my Father's world," was published shortly after his tragic death in Naples, Italy, 1901, in a post-humous collection of his poems, *Thoughts for Every Day Living,* prepared by his wife and Miss Sanford. Those, who knew Doctor Babcock well, have felt that these lines were truly expressive of his joyous Christian life. He was pastor of the Brick Presbyterian Church, New York city, until his death, having previously served Presbyterian churches in Lockport and Baltimore. Born in 1858, he was a graduate of Syracuse University, 1879.

TUNE: "Terra Beata" is a lilting traditional English folk song, which has been successfully arranged in hymn-tune form.

177. In Heavenly Love Abiding

Tune: *"Day of Rest"*

Anna L. Waring   James W. Elliott

In 1850, the year of the publication of her *Hymns and Meditations,* Miss Anna Lætitia Waring wrote her hymn, "In heavenly love abiding," for the book in which it bears the title, "Safety in God." Its scriptural reference is Psalms 23, 4: "I will fear no evil, for thou art with me." (See No. 182.)

TUNE: James W. Elliott, born in England, 1833, and residing in London, was organist and choirmaster in St. Mark's Church, Hamilton Terrace. He wrote his tune, "Day of Rest," for Bishop Christopher Wordsworth's hymn, "O day of rest and gladness," and it derives its title from that first line.

178. When Winds Are Raging O'er the Upper Ocean

Tune: *"Clifton"*

Harriet Beecher Stowe   Uzziah C. Burnap

Mrs. Harriet Beecher Stowe (1812-1896), the daughter of the Rev. Dr. Lyman Beecher, and sister of the Rev. Dr. Henry Ward Beecher—each of them famous American clergymen—achieved her greatest fame through the publication of her anti-slavery novel, *Uncle Tom's Cabin,* in *The National Era,* 1852, and subsequently in book form. In 1833 she was wed to the Rev. Dr. Calvin E. Stowe, professor of Languages and Biblical Literature in Lane Seminary, Cincinnati, Ohio, of which institution her father had become president, the year before. Her brother, then pastor of Plymouth Church, Brooklyn, in 1855 edited a hymnal, *The Plymouth Collection,* in which was included her hymn, "When winds are raging on the upper ocean."

TUNE: The tune, "Clifton," was composed by Uzziah C. Burnap, a New England composer. He has written many hymn-tunes which in recent years have come into circulation in the standard hymnals.

179. O Love Divine That Stooped to Share

TUNE: *"Zephyr"*

OLIVER WENDELL HOLMES

WILLIAM B. BRADBURY

Following the success of his famous book, *The Autocrat of the Breakfast Table,* Dr. Oliver Wendell Holmes, physician, poet, essayist, published a similar book, *The Professor at the Breakfast Table,* in which was included his hymn (1859), "O Love divine that stoop'st to share" (or "stooped," as our present version hath it). He entitled it, "A Hymn of Trust."

TUNE: "Zephyr" is one of the many successful hymn-tunes composed by William B. Bradbury. (See No. 325.)

180. Thou Hidden Source of Calm Repose

TUNE: *"Pater Omnium"*

CHARLES WESLEY

H. J. E. HOLMES

Under the heading, "Hymns for Believers. For the Morning," Charles Wesley's hymn, "Thou hidden Source of calm repose," was first published in the Wesley's *Hymns and Sacred Poems,* 1749. The last four words of the hymn were originally "my heaven in hell" (instead of "my all in all"). Stevenson, the English hymnologist, in commenting upon the antithesis which Wesley developed in these lines, said: "Christ is the Christian's rest in toil, his ease in pain, his peace in war, his gain in loss, his liberty in bondage, and last of all comes this marvelous climax—his heaven in hell." (See No. 100.)

TUNE: "Pater Omnium" (See No. 48).

181. Jesus, I My Cross Have Taken

TUNE: *"Ellesdie"*

HENRY F. LYTE   JOHANN C. W. A. MOZART

Julian makes this comment upon the life of the Rev. Dr. Henry F. Lyte, author of "Jesus, I my cross have taken," which expressed somewhat the spirit of the hymn:

In 1817 he removed to Marazion, in Cornwall. There, in 1818, he underwent a great spiritual change, which shaped and influenced the whole of his after-life, the immediate cause being the illness and death of a brother clergyman. Lyte says of him: "He died happy under the belief that though he had deeply erred, there was *One* whose death and sufferings would atone for his delinquencies, and be accepted for all that he had incurred"; and concerning himself he adds: "I was greatly affected by the whole matter, and brought to look at life and its issue with a different eye than before; and I began to study my Bible, and preach in another manner than I had previously done." (See No. 208.)

TUNE: "Ellesdie" (See No. 137).

182. Father, I Know That All My Life

TUNE: *"St. Bede"*

ANNA L. WARING   JOHN B. DYKES

Miss Anna Lætitia Waring, born in southern Wales, 1820, published her *Hymns and Meditations* in London, 1853, and it was republished by The Association of Friends for the Diffusion of Religious and Useful Knowledge, ten years later in Philadelphia. This work contained her hymn, "Father, I know that all my life," and it was headed, "My times are in thy hands" (Psalm 31, 15).

TUNE: "St. Bede," named for one of the English churches, was composed by the Rev. Dr. John Bacchus Dykes. (See No. 113.)

183. O Thou in Whose Presence

TUNE: *"Meditation"*

JOSEPH SWAIN   FREEMAN LEWIS

The Rev. Joseph Swain, English Baptist minister of the East Street Church, Walworth, published in 1791 (the year he entered upon his five years ministry in this church) an edition of his *Redemption, a Poem in Five Books,* which contained his hymn, "O Thou in whose presence my soul takes delight." It was written during a long illness. Five years later he died.

TUNE: Freeman Lewis, American writer of the tune, "Meditation," was born in 1780 and died in 1859. He edited the music collection, *The Beauties of Harmony,* Pittsburgh, 1813. Lewis was a surveyor at Uniontown, Pennsylvania, as well as a musician.

184. He That Is Down Needs Fear No Fall

TUNE: *"St. Hugh"*

JOHN BUNYAN

English Traditional

John Bunyan's hymn, "He that is down needs fear no fall," is taken from the Second Part of *The Pilgrim's Progress,* 1684, without alteration. It is the Shepherd Boy's Song, which Christiana and her friends heard as they passed into the Valley of Humiliation, when it was being sung by a boy "in very mean cloaths," who was tending his father's sheep.

TUNE: "St. Hugh" is a hymn-tune arrangement of an old English traditional melody, which in quaintness and strength peculiarly matches the spirit of Bunyan's hymn.

185. O Love That Wilt Not Let Me Go

TUNE: *"Margaret"*

GEORGE MATHESON

ALBERT L. PEACE

The Rev. Dr. George Matheson, blind since he was fifteen years old, became one of the most honored clergymen in the Church of Scotland, and through his preaching, his lectures (Baird Lecturer, 1881, and St. Giles Lecturer, 1882), his many books and poems, he exerted a wide influence. He once told the story of his hymn, "O Love that wilt not let me go," which, he said was

written in the Manse of my former parish (Innellan, Argyleshire) one summer evening in 1882. It was composed with extreme rapidity; it seemed to me that its construction occupied only a few minutes, and I felt myself rather in the position of one who was being dictated to than of an original artist. I was suffering from extreme mental distress, and the hymn was the fruit of pain.

The refusal of his fiancée to marry him because of his blindness is sometimes repeated as the reason for his writing the hymn; but this is not true.

TUNE: Dr. Albert L. Peace, born in 1845, was organist in the Glascow Cathedral, 1879. His tune, "Margaret," is but one of many he composed. It is sometimes called "St. Margaret."

186.   I Bow My Forehead to the Dust

TUNE: *"Amesbury"*

JOHN G. WHITTIER   UZZIAH C. BURNAP

The Tent on the Beach and Other Poems was the title of a book of poems by John G. Whittier, published in 1867. From this poem of twenty-two stanzas on the Eternal Goodness are taken the lines, "I bow my forehead in the dust," though they have in the hymn been rearranged in order.   (See No. 2.)

TUNE: "Amesbury" was composed by the American musician, Uzziah C. Burnap.   (See No. 178.)

187.   Lead, Kindly Light

TUNE: *"Lux Benigna"*

JOHN H. NEWMAN   JOHN B. DYKES

In his *Apologia Pro Vita Sua,* 1864, Cardinal Newman tells the story of how as a clergyman in the Church of England, returning from Rome, and convalescing from a serious illness, he came to write "Lead, kindly light." Detained at Palermo for three weeks, awaiting a ship,

at last I got off in an orange boat bound for Marseilles. We were becalmed a whole week in the Straits of Bonifacio. Then it was that I wrote the lines "Lead, kindly light" (June 16, 1833), which have since become well known. I was writing verses the whole time of my passage. At length I got to Marseilles, and set off for England. The fatigue of travelling was too much for me, and I was laid up for several days at Lyons. At last I got off again and did not stop night or day till I reached England, and my mother's house.

TUNE: The Rev. Dr. John Bacchus Dykes on August 29, 1865, as his diary tells us, "began writing a tune for 'Lead, Kindly Light,' " which had occurred to him during a walk along the Strand in London. It was published in the Rev. D. T. Barry's *Psalms and Hymns,* 1867, with the title, "St. Oswald," the name of the church where Doctor Dykes was then serving as vicar in Durham. But the tune later was renamed with a Latin phrase from the hymn's first line, "Lux Benigna," which means "Kindly Light." Newman, author of the hymn, used to say: "It is not the hymn, but the tune that has gained the popularity. The tune is Dykes', and Doctor Dykes is a great master." (See No. 113.)

188. Jesus, Lover of My Soul
TUNES: *"Hollingside" "Martyn"*

CHARLES WESLEY

JOHN B. DYKES
SIMEON B. MARSH

Charles Wesley has been styled the greatest hymn-writer in the English language; and many have regarded "Jesus, Lover of my soul," as his greatest hymn. His brother, John Wesley, would not admit it in the Wesleyan Methodist hymn-book; but, in spite of some of its obvious defects, it has attained great popularity and usefulness. Wesley wrote it in 1739, and the next year it was published under the title, "In Temptation," in *Hymns and Sacred Poems.* The stories of its origin during a mob attack, or when a hawk flew in the window, are scarcely to be credited. (See No. 100.)

FIRST TUNE: Doctor Dykes, composer of the tune, "Hollingside," right after his marriage in 1850, settled in Hollingside Cottage, a short way from Durham. While living there, he composed the tune, which bears the name of the first joint home of Doctor and Mrs. Dykes. (See No. 113.)

SECOND TUNE: Simeon Butler Marsh (1798-1875), a native of Wethersfield, Connecticut, composed his tune, "Martyn," in the fall of 1834, while traveling on horseback from Amsterdam to Johnstown, setting it first to John Newton's "Mary at her Saviour's tomb," to which it was published in *The Plymouth Collection* by Henry Ward Beecher, 1855. Dr. Thomas Hastings first used it to "Jesus, Lover of my soul." Marsh was a prominent leader of choral singing and an organist in Sherburne, New York.

189.   I Sought the Lord, and Afterward
TUNE: *"Artavia"*
ANONYMOUS   EDWARD J. HOPKINS

The author of the hymn, "I sought the Lord and afterward," is not known; but it was probably first printed in *The Pilgrim Hymnal,* 1904.

TUNE: The composer of "Artavia," was the famous English organist and hymnal editor, Dr. Edward J. Hopkins. (See No. 18.)

190.   How Firm a Foundation
TUNE: *"Portuguese Hymn"*
GEORGE KEITH   COMPOSER UNKNOWN

The original title of "How firm a foundation" in Rippon's *Selection of Hymns from the Best Authors,* etc., 1787, was "Exceeding great and precious promises." It was signed "K—"; but it is not known definitely for what name the initial stands. Julian says it was "Keen," others say "Kirkham" or "George Keith." R. Keene, who composed the tune, "Gerard," to these words, was precentor in Dr. Rippon's Baptist church in London, and possibly he wrote also the words; though more probably they were written by George Keith.

TUNE: "Portuguese Hymn" (See No. 55).

191.   Who Fathoms the Eternal Thought
TUNE: *"Fingal"*
JOHN G. WHITTIER   JAMES S. ANDERSON

The hymn, "Who fathoms the eternal thought," was taken from stanza four *et seq.* of John G. Whittier's *The Tent on the Beach.* (See Nos. 2 and 186.)

TUNE: James Smith Anderson, born in Crail, Fife, was educated in Edinburgh and Glasgow, Scotland; and in 1878 he received the degree of Mus. Bac. at Oxford University. He has been organist and choirmaster in a number of Edinburgh churches, has written many hymn-tunes, and helped edit the *Church Hymnary.* His tune, "Fingal," was first published in *The Scottish Hymnal,* 1885, to the hymn, "I am not worthy, Holy Lord."

192. O For a Closer Walk with God

TUNE: *"Beatitudo"*

WILLIAM COWPER

JOHN B. DYKES

The second edition of R. Conyers's *Collection of Psalms and Hymns,* 1772, contained the beautiful hymn of the poet, William Cowper, "O for a closer walk with God." In the *Olney Hymns* it was entitled, "Walking with God." Cowper's dependence upon Mrs. Mary Unwin, who cared for him tenderly when his mind became unbalanced, was pathetic. She had been quite ill, shortly before this hymn was written, and it had brought him to exclaim: "O for no will but the will of my heavenly Father!" Of the lines of this hymn he wrote to his aunt: "I began to compose them yesterday morning before daybreak, but I fell asleep at the end of the first two lines. When I awaked again, the third and fourth verses were whispered to my heart in a way I have often experienced." (See No. 114.)

TUNE: In 1875 the tune, "Beatitudo," was composed by the Rev. Dr. John Bacchus Dykes. (See No. 113.)

193. Jesus, Saviour, Pilot Me

TUNE: *"Pilot"*

EDWARD HOPPER

JOHN E. GOULD

The Rev. Edward Hopper, pastor of the Presbyterian Church of the Sea and Land, New York city, was asked to write a hymn for the anniversary of the American Seamen's Friend Society of that city on May 10, 1880, in the Broadway Tabernacle. He read instead, however, a hymn which he had written for the *Sailor's Magazine* in 1871, "Jesus, Saviour, pilot me," which had appeared anonymously there and also in the *Baptist Praise Book,* 1871.

TUNE: John Edgar Gould, born in Bangor, Maine, 1820, composed much music, managed a music store in New York, and edited many hymnals, such as *The Modern Harp,* 1846, *Harmonia Sacra,* 1851, and *Songs of Gladness,* 1869. After living in Bergen Heights, New Jersey, and in Philadelphia, he went abroad for his health in 1874, but died in 1875 at Algiers.

194. They Who Seek the Throne of Grace

TUNE: *"Hendon"*

OLIVER HOLDEN   H. A. CESAR MILAN

Oliver Holden, who wrote the tune, "Coronation," was a Charlestown (Massachusetts) music publisher. Among the many music books he edited was *The Young Convert's Companion. Being a Collection of Hymns for the Use of Conference Meetings,* Boston, 1806. Nineteen of his hymns are in this collection; and one of them, entitled, "Secret Prayer," was the hymn, "They who seek the throne of grace." It has been greatly altered from the original, but its present form preserves the spirit of Holden's lines. (See No. 78.)

TUNE: Dr. Henry Abraham Cesar Milan, born in Geneva, 1787, was a famous French preacher and for a time preached in the cathedral at Geneva. His change of doctrinal belief in 1818 led to his dismissal from the Established Church, but he continued preaching until his death in 1864. He wrote many hymns, as well as tunes, among the latter being the popular hymn-tune, "Hendon."

195. Come Unto Me

TUNE: *"Henley"*

CATHERINE H. ESLING   LOWELL MASON

Miss Catherine H. Watterman, member of the Protestant Episcopal Church, in 1839 wrote "Come unto Me, when shadows darkly gather," and it was published that year in an annual periodical, *The Christian Keepsake,* in which its title was "Come Unto Me." The following year she married George J. Esling of Philadelphia. The original hymn was three times as long as its present form.

TUNE: The hymn-tune, "Henley," was composed by Lowell Mason in 1854. (See No. 21.)

196. My God, Is Any Hour So Sweet

TUNE: *"Almsgiving"*

CHARLOTTE ELLIOTT   JOHN B. DYKES

Miss Charlotte Elliott (1789-1871) was an invalid for over a half century, but from her sick chamber she sang some of our tenderest Christian hymns, such as "Just as I am without one plea" and this hymn, "My God, is any hour so sweet." The latter gives to us an insight into that secret prayer life that sustained her so marvelously through all her trials and sufferings. It was published in her book, *Hours of Sorrow Cheered and Comforted,* 1836. (See No. 102.)

TUNE: Doctor Dykes's tune, "Almsgiving," was so named because he wrote it first to the hymn, "O Lord of heaven and earth and sea," to which it is still sung. (See No. 113.)

197. From Every Stormy Wind That Blows

TUNE: *"Retreat"*

HUGH STOWELL   THOMAS HASTINGS

The Rev. Hugh Stowell was rector of Christ Church, Salford, England, when he was appointed Hon. Canon of Chester Cathedral. His poem, entitled, "Peace at the Mercy Seat," beginning; "From every stormy wind that blows," was published in *The Winter's Wreath, a Collection of original contributions in Prose and Verse,* London and Liverpool, 1828. This was an annual publication from 1828 to 1832. It later appeared in his *Psalms and Hymns,* 1831.

TUNE: The tune, "Retreat," by Dr. Thomas Hastings was written especially for Hugh Stowell's "From every stormy wind that blows," with its memorable third line, "There is a calm, a sure retreat." It was this last word which gave the tune its title. (See No. 43.)

198. Prayer Is the Soul's Sincere Desire

TUNE: *"Lambeth"*

JAMES MONTGOMERY   ANONYMOUS

The Rev. E. Bickersteth in 1818 requested the poet-editor, James Montgomery, to write a poem to be included in the former's forthcoming book, *Treatise on Prayer.* The result was what Montgomery called "the most attractive hymn I ever wrote," "Prayer is the soul's sincere desire." It was first printed that year in a broadsheet with three others of Montgomery's hymns, "Thou, God, art a consuming fire," "Lord, teach us how to pray aright," and "What shall we ask of God in prayer"; and they were used by the Sunday schools of Sheffield, England, Montgomery's home. (See No. 51.)

TUNE: The tune, "Lambeth," is anonymous; though it is sometimes attributed to William A. F. Schulthes, 1871.

199. My Soul, Be on Thy Guard

TUNE: "Laban"

GEORGE HEATH   LOWELL MASON

The Rev. George Heath was pastor of the Honiton Presbyterian Church in Devon, England, in 1770. In 1781 his hymn on "Fight the Good Fight of Faith" appeared in his book, *Hymns and Poetic Essays Sacred to the Public and Private Worship of the Deity, and to Religious and Christian Improvement,* 1781. Forced out of the Presbyterian Church for misconduct, he later became a Unitarian clergyman. Duffield has said of this:

It is a striking commentary on his hymn that its author should have failed in the very mode against which his stirring trumpet blast ought effectually to have warned him. But let us be charitable and hope that this was one of the fruits of true repentance, for the hymn was published in 1781.

TUNE: Lowell Mason in 1830 composed his stirring tune, "Laban." (See No. 21.)

200. Stand Fast for Christ Thy Saviour

TUNE: "Alford"

WALTER J. MATHAMS   JOHN B. DYKES

The Rev. Walter J. Mathams, an English clergyman, in 1913 wrote the hymn, "Stand fast for Christ thy Saviour." He was born in London, 1851, spent his boyhood days at sea, and later became educated for the Baptist ministry, serving churches at Preston, Falkirk and Birmingham. After three years' service as chaplain to the British Army in Egypt, he entered the ministry of the Church of Scotland, serving at Stronsay and Mallaig

Mission. In 1919 he retired. He has written many books and some stirring hymns.

TUNE: The tune, "Alford," by the Rev. Dr. John Bacchus Dykes, was named for Dean Alford of Canterbury Cathedral, who wrote the hymn, "Ten thousand times ten thousand," to which the tune is often sung. (See No. 113.)

201. My Jesus, as Thou Wilt

Tune: *"Jewett"*

Benjamin Schmolke
Translated by Jane Borthwick   From Carl Maria von Weber

The Rev. Benjamin Schmolke (1672-1737) was for thirty-five years pastor of a Lutheran Church at Schweianitz in Germany, first as assistant to his father, and then later as the chief pastor. He and his church suffered severe persecutions from the Counter-Reformation movement. But in the spirit of his hymn, "My Jesus, as Thou wilt," he suffered courageously and became known as a very "popular and useful preacher."

TUNE: The hymn-tune, "Jewett," is taken from the opera, "Der Freischütz," by the famous German composer, Carl Maria von Weber. (See No. 29.)

202. Come, Ye Disconsolate

Tune: *"Alma"*

Thomas Moore, Thomas Hastings   Samuel Webbe

The famous Irish poet, Thomas Moore, was born in Dublin in 1779 and in that same city was graduated from Trinity College. Of the thirty-two poems in his *Sacred Songs,* published in 1816, one was entitled "Come, Ye Disconsolate." The first two stanzas of this poem, plus a new stanza, probably written by the American hymnist, Thomas Hastings, appeared in Hastings and Lowell Mason's book, *Spiritual Songs,* 1831, practically in the form of our present hymn of the same title. Moore was a musician. Though his life did not measure up to Christian standards, twelve of his hymns, taken from

Sacred Songs, have been widely used by the church. (See No. 48.)

TUNE: The tune, "Alma," was taken from a larger composition by the Roman Catholic organist in London, Samuel Webbe. (See No. 84.)

203. My God, My Father, While I Stray

TUNE: *"Hanford"*

CHARLOTTE ELLIOTT   ARTHUR S. SULLIVAN

Charlotte Elliott (see No. 102) published in 1834 a group of poems, written in her sick chamber, under the title, *The Invalid's Hymn Book;* and the hymn, "My God, my Father, while I stray," which first appeared in this collection, is eloquent of the conditions of suffering under which she wrote and of the sweet spirit in which she bore them. The fifth stanza of her hymn is usually omitted:

> Should pining sickness waste away
> My life in premature decay,
> My Father! still I strive to say,
> "Thy will be done!"

TUNE: The tune, "Hanford," like the tune, "St. Gertrude" (see No. 144), was composed by Sir Arthur S. Sullivan at the home of Mrs. Gertrude Clay-Ker-Seymer in Hanford, Dorsetshire, where the composer was often a welcome guest for weeks at a time. This tune, however, takes its title from the town, and not from the hostess. (See No. 73.)

204. For All the Saints

TUNE: *"Sarum"*

WILLIAM W. HOW   JOSEPH BARNBY

Earl Nelson, a layman, gave the first publication of the hymn, "For all the saints," by Bishop William Walsham How of the Church of England, in his book, *Hymn for Saints' Day, and Other Hymns,* 1864. Its eleven stanzas are here reduced to six. As the title implies, this was written especially for Saints' Day, and has become the most popular of the many hymns of this gifted hymnist, which are in common use. (See No. 88.)

TUNE: The tune, "Sarum," was composed by Sir Joseph Barnby. (See No. 14.) It derives its title from the *Sarum Breviary,* an office book of the canonical hours, which was in use in England before the Reformation.

205. Jesus, the Very Thought of Thee

TUNE: *"St. Agnes"*

BERNARD OF CLAIRVAUX
Translated by EDWARD CASWALL

JOHN B. DYKES

The translation by the Rev. Edward Caswall of the famous Latin hymn, "Jesu, dulcis memoria," first appeared in *Lyra Catholica,* 1848, and was probably composed after Caswall had left the ministry of the Church of England to enter the Roman Catholic Church. Some doubt has been raised as to the authorship of the original Latin hymn, though tradition has long assigned it to Bernard of Clairvaux, the famous monk of the twelfth century, who swayed the acts of kings and popes, changed the course of European history, and became recognized (to use Luther's phrase) as "the greatest monk that ever lived." (See No. 14.)

TUNE: "St. Agnes" (See No. 113).

206. Jesus Calls Us, O'er the Tumult

TUNE: *"Jude"*

CECIL F. ALEXANDER

WILLIAM H. JUDE

"He saith unto them, Follow me" is Matthew's description of the calling of Peter and Andrew by their Master at the Sea of Galilee (Mathew 4, 19); and Mrs. Cecil F. Alexander, wife of the Bishop of Derry in Ireland, had this passage upon her heart when she wrote: "Jesus calls us, o'er the tumult." This is evidenced by the omitted second stanza,

> As of old St. Andrew heard it
>   By the Galilean lake,
> Turned from home, and toil, and kindred,
>   Leaving all for His dear sake.

The Society for the Propagation of Christian Knowledge first printed it in their hymn-book in 1852. (See No. 59.)

TUNE: The tune, "Jude," sometimes called "Galilee," was composed in 1887 by the English composer and organist, William Herbert Jude, who was born in 1851. He has published many hymn-tunes.

207. Praise the Lord, His Glories Show

TUNE: *"Llanfair"*

HENRY F. LYTE   ROBERT WILLIAMS

In the Rev. Henry F. Lyte's *Spirit of the Psalms,* 1834, was first printed the hymn, "Praise the Lord, His glories show," which is Lyte's happy translation of Psalm 150. It later appeared in a revised version of the same book, 1836, in slightly altered form; but our hymn, as here presented, conforms to the original version. His revision began the second stanza with this couplet:

> Earth to heaven exalt the strain,
> Send it, heaven, to earth again.
>
> (See No. 208.)

TUNE: Robert Williams (1781-1821), a native of Anglesey, was a blind basket-maker and musician. His tune, "Llanfair," first appeared in J. Parry's *Peroriaeth Hyfryd,* 1837, a Welsh hymnal, and was harmonized by John Roberts of Henllan.

208. Praise, My Soul, the King of Heaven

TUNE: *"Praise My Soul"*

HENRY F. LYTE   JOHN GOSS

The Rev. Henry F. Lyte was born near Kelso, Scotland, 1793, was graduated from Trinity College, Dublin, 1814, and became a clergyman of the Church of England in 1815. "Praise, my soul, the King of heaven" is another of his psalm translations, appearing in his *Spirit of the Psalms,* 1834. (See No. 207.) It is his version of Psalm 103; and, as Canon John Julian says, "is one of his most successful paraphrases of the Psalms, and is more jubilant than is usually the case with his renderings." At the time of publication of these psalms, Lyte was Perpetual Curate of Lower Brixham, Devonshire. He held this post until his death, November 20, 1847. (See No. 31.)

TUNE: The hymn-tune, "Praise My Soul," composed by Sir John Goss, was first published in Brown-Borthwick's *Supplemental Tune-Book,* 1869. Born in 1800 at Fareham, Goss became famous as the organist of St. Paul's Cathedral, London, as musical editor of *Parochial Psalmody,* 1926, Malan's *Hymns of Redemption,* 1838, *Church Psalter and Hymn-Book,* 1854, etc., and as composer of much fine church music. He died in 1880.

209. Peace, Perfect Peace

TUNE: *"Pax Tecum"*

EDWARD H. BICKERSTETH   G. T. CALDBECK

The Rev. Edward Henry Bickersteth (afterwards Bishop of Exeter, Church of England) was the father of the Rev. Dr. S. Bickersteth, who once told the story of the writing of this hymn to Canon Julian in the following words:

This hymn was written by Bishop Edward Henry Bickersteth, D.D., while he was spending his summer holiday in Harrogate in the year of 1875, in a house facing the Stray, lent to him by his friend, Mr. Armitage, then Vicar of Casterton.

On a Sunday morning in August, the Vicar of Harrogate, Canon Gibbon, happened to preach from the text, "Thou wilt keep him in perfect peace whose mind is stayed on Thee," and alluded to the fact that in the Hebrew the words are "Peace, peace," twice repeated, and happily translated in the 1611 translation by the phrase, "Perfect peace." This sermon set my father's mind working on the subject. He always found it easiest to express in verse whatever subject was uppermost in his mind, so that when on the afternoon of that Sunday he visited an aged and dying relative, Archdeacon Hill of Liverpool, and found him somewhat troubled in mind, it was natural to him to express in verse the spiritual comfort which he desired to convey. Taking up a sheet of paper he then and there wrote down the hymn just exactly as it stands, and read it to this dying Christian. (See No. 6.)

TUNE: George T. Caldbeck, an amateur musician in England, composed his tune, "Pax Tecum," in 1876 to Bishop Bickersteth's hymn, "Peace, perfect peace." Its Latin title means, "Peace with thee." Charles J. Vincent harmonized the tune for Caldbeck and it has ever since been associated with this one hymn.

210.   Dear Lord and Father of Mankind

TUNE: *"Elton"*

JOHN G. WHITTIER   FREDERICK C. MAKER

In 1872 the American poet, John G. Whittier (1807-1892), wrote a poem entitled, "The Brewing of Soma," consisting of seventeen stanzas; and this was published in his *Complete Poetical Works,* 1876. From this poem has been made our hymn, "Dear Lord and Father of mankind," by taking the twelfth, thirteenth, fourteenth, sixteenth and seventeenth stanzas. In this form it appeared in Horder's *Congregational Hymns,* 1884. (See No. 2.)

TUNE: The tune, "Elton," was composed by Frederick C. Maker. (See No. 112.)

211.   God Is My Strong Salvation

TUNE: *"Chenies"*

JAMES MONTGOMERY   TIMOTHY R. MATTHEWS

In 1822 James Montgomery published his *Songs of Zion,* which is based on a portion of Psalm 27, "The Lord is my light and my salvation," *et seq.* All of the poems in this collection are from the psalms, including his popular version of Psalm 23, "The Lord is my Shepherd, no want shall I know." (See No. 51.)

TUNE: The Rev. Timothy R. Matthews, born in 1826, became a clergyman in the Church of England after his graduation from Cambridge University in 1853. He composed many hymn-tunes, among them "Chenies."

212.   Children of the Heavenly King

TUNE: *"Vienna"*

JOHN CENNICK   JUSTIN H. KNECHT

The author of *Sacred Hymns for the Children of God, in the Day of Their Pilgrimage* by J. C., London, 1742, was John Cennick (1718-1755), a native of Berkshire, England, who at the time he wrote most of these hymns was a Methodist preacher, active in the Wesleyan revival. In this volume was first published his hymn, "Children of the heavenly King," which has been widely used in Christian worship ever since. Cennick once wrote concerning his own hymns: "I would not have any who read these hymns look to find either good poetry or fine language, for indeed there is none." Hatfield has commented upon the truth of this passage, adding that "the few hymns from his pen that are now used have been considerably modified to fit them for the service of song, and are known at present almost wholly in these altered forms."

TUNE: The tune, "Vienna," by the German composer, Justin H. Knecht, was named for the European city which he often visited. (See No. 101.)

213. My God, I Thank Thee, Who Hast Made

TUNE: *"Fowler"*

ADELAIDE A. PROCTER ROBERT G. McCUTCHAN

Legends and Lyrics, a Book of Verse by Miss Adelaide Anne Procter, daughter of Bryan Wiler Procter (Barry Cornwall), was published in 1858, and contained the poem, beginning, "I thank Thee, O my God, who made," in six stanzas, from which has been taken our hymn of five stanzas, beginning, "My God, I thank Thee, who hast made." In his *Hymnal Companion,* 1876, Bishop Edward H. Bickersteth has said of it: "This most beautiful hymn by A. A. Procter (1858) touches the chord of thankfulness in trial, as perhaps no other hymn does, and is thus most useful for the visitation of the sick." (See No. 34.)

TUNE: The title of the tune, "Fowler," by Robert G. McCutchan, was taken from the middle name of the hymnal editor, Carl Fowler Price, who in turn was named for Bishop Charles H. Fowler of the Methodist Episcopal Church. (See No. 105.)

214. Ye Watchers and Ye Holy Ones

TUNE: *"Vigili et Sancti"*

ATHELSTAN RILEY COLOGNE, 1623

John Athelstan Laurie Riley, M.A., born in London, August 10, 1858, and a graduate of Eton and Pembroke

HAND BOOK TO STANDARD HYMNS AND GOSPEL SONGS

College, Oxford, was one of the compilers of *The English Hymnal,* that most important hymnal of the Church of England which appeared in 1906 and has seriously challenged the supremacy of *Hymns Ancient and Modern* in the churches of that denomination. To this book he contributed his hymn on "Universal Praise to God," beginning, "Ye watchers and ye holy ones"; and also two other original hymns, seven translations from the Latin and one from the Greek. He is now a resident of the Isle of Jersey.

TUNE: A melody, found in an old collection, published in Cologne, 1623, has been modernized in harmony and adapted as a hymn-tune, "Vigili et Sancti," taking its Latin title ("Watchers and Holy Ones") from Riley's more recent hymn, "Ye watchers and ye holy ones."

215. Speak, Lord, in the Stillness

TUNE: *"The Quiet Hour"*

E. MAY GRIMES

J. B. NIELD

E. May Grimes, author of the hymn, "Speak, Lord, in the stillness," is a resident of California. The hymn found its first hymnal publication in *Standard Hymns and Gospel Songs,* 1930.

TUNE: "The Quiet Hour" was especially written for Miss Grimes's hymn, "Speak, Lord in the stillness," by J. B. Nield, an organist in Hollywood, California.

216. Rejoice, the Lord Is King!

TUNE: *"Jubilate"*

CHARLES WESLEY. Altered

HORATIO PARKER

Charles Wesley's hymn, "Rejoice, the Lord is King," appeared in his 1746 book, *Hymns on Our Lord's Resurrection,* and is based on Phil. 4, 4: "Rejoice in the Lord always; and again I say, Rejoice." (See No. 100.)

TUNE: The tune, "Jubilate," was composed by Horatio William Parker, one of America's greatest composers. Born in Auburndale, Massachusetts, on September 15, 1863, he died at Cedarhurst, New York, December 18, 1919. The son of an architect, he studied music with the famous G. W. Chadwick, became a great organist, playing at Holy Trinity, New York, and Trinity, Boston; was at the head of the music department of Yale University, and made a great name as composer of "Hora Novissima," "The Dream King," "Legend of St. Christopher," "Mona," "Fairyland" and a large number of lesser compositions in church music and other fields. He edited a tune edition of the Protestant Episcopal *Hymnal,* published in New York, 1903.

217. Blest Be the Tie That Binds
TUNE: *"Dennis"*

JOHN FAWCETT   HANS G. NAEGELI

In *Singers and Songs of the Church,* 1869, Miller has told us this interesting story of the origin of the hymn, "Blest be the tie that binds":

> This favorite hymn is said to have been written in 1772, to commemorate the determination of its author to remain with his attached people at Wainsgate. The farewell sermon was preached, the wagons were loaded, when love and tears prevailed, and Dr. Fawcett sacrificed the attractions of a London pulpit to the affection of his poor but devoted flock.

The Rev. Dr. John Fawcett (1739-1817), a native of Yorkshire, was at the age of sixteen converted through the preaching of George Whitefield, joined the Methodists, and later the Baptists. He began his ministry as pastor of the Baptist Church at Wainsgate, near Hebden Bridge, Yorkshire. It was in 1772 that he was called to London as pastor of Carter's Lane. He later declined the presidency of the Baptist Academy at Bristol. They built a new chapel for him at Hebden Bridge, where he served all the years of his ministry. This hymn, under the title, "Brotherly Love," was printed first in Doctor Fawcett's *Hymns Adapted to the Circumstances of Public Worship and Private Devotion,* 1782.

TUNE: The melody of "Dennis" first appeared as a hymn tune, set to "How gentle God's commands," in *The*

Psaltery, 1845. Lowell Mason arranged it from a tune by Hans G. Naegeli, who was born in Zurich, 1768, and managed there a publishing house, and later edited a musical periodical. He died in Zurich, 1836.

218. Praise to Our God, Who With Love

TUNE: *"Curfew"*

HERBERT B. GRAY   FREDERICK C. MAKER

The Rev. Dr. Herbert Branston Gray, the son of Thomas Gray, was born on April 22, 1851, in London, and was graduated from Winchester and Queen's College, Oxford. He became assistant master at his old school, Westminster, 1875; head-master of Louth Grammar School, 1878; head-master of Bradford College in 1880 and warden in 1881. Twelve years later he wrote his hymn, "Praise to our God, who with love never swerving," to be sung at the end of the college term, 1893; and it was printed in the *Bradford College Supplement to Hymns Ancient and Modern,* 1895.

TUNE: The tune, "Curfew," is by Frederick C. Maker. (See No. 112.)

219. Through the Night of Doubt and Sorrow

TUNE: *"Gade"*

BERNARD S. INGEMANN   Arranged from Schumann's
Translated by S. BARING-GOULD   "Norwegian Folk Song"

Denmark's favorite poet, Professor Bernard S. Ingemann (1789-1862), of the Academy of Sorö, Zealand, Denmark, composed the original Danish hymn, "Igjennem Nat og Traengsel," in 1825 when he was professor of the Danish Literature and Language. From this hymn the Rev. S. Baring-Gould of the Church of England made the English translation, "Through the night of doubt and sorrow," which was published in *The People's Hymnal,* 1867, and later in a revised and improved form in *Hymns Ancient and Modern,* 1875. (See No. 28.)

TUNE: It is fitting that this Scandinavian hymn should be sung to the Norwegian Folk Song, which the German composer, Robert Schumann, made popular. (See No. 19.)

220. O God, Our Help in Ages Past

TUNE: *"St. Anne"*

ISAAC WATTS   WILLIAM CROFT

"Our God, our help in ages past," as this hymn was originally written by the Rev. Dr. Isaac Watts, was the first part of his translation of Psalm 90, and under the title, "Man Frail and God Eternal," it appeared in his *Psalms of David Imitated in the Language of the New Testament, And apply'd to the Christian State and Worship,* 1719. The pattern of the hymn follows a form, familiar in many of the psalms: 1. Thesis, contemplation of the greatness of God, first three stanzas; 2. Antithesis, of man's weakness, fourth stanza; 3. Synthesis, man's weakness finds its complement in the eternal help of God, last stanza. (See No. 174.)

TUNE: "St. Anne" (See No. 91).

221. Another Year Is Dawning

TUNE: *"Carmina"*

FRANCES R. HAVERGAL   Arranged from F. FLOTOW

Miss Frances Ridley Havergal (1836-1879) wrote her New Year's Hymn, "Another year is dawning," in 1874, and published it as a New Year's card; and in the same year it appeared in her book, *Under the Surface.* One writer has said that "her poems are permeated with the fragrance of her passionate love of Jesus." This shines through these lines, penned five years before she died. (See No. 110.)

TUNE: Baron Friedrich von Flotow, born in 1812, was a German composer of operas. "Martha," his best-known opera, he wrote in 1847. He died in 1883. From one of his melodies has been arranged the hymn-tune, entitled "Carmina," which is the Latin for "Songs."

222.   Ring Out, Wild Bells, to the Wild, Wild Sky

TUNE: *"Wild Bells"*

ALFRED TENNYSON   HENRY LAHEE

Alfred Lord Tennyson, son of the Rev. G. C. Tennyson, rector of Somersby, Lincolnshire, in the year that he was appointed Poet Laureate, 1850, published his great poem, *In Memoriam,* and from this poem were taken the lines beginning, "Ring out, wild bells, to the wild, wild sky," as well as the hymn, "Strong Son of God, immortal Love." The whole poem was a memorial to the friend of his youth, Arthur H. Hallam, who died in Vienna, 1833.

TUNE: Henry Lahee, born in 1826, was a prominent organist in London, and a choral leader, as well as a composer. In his tune, "Wild Bells," he sets ringing in his musical chimes what Tennyson has so joyously described in his poem, "Ring out, wild bells."

223.   Break, New-Born Year, on Glad Eyes Break

TUNE: *"Warwick"*

THOMAS H. GILL   SAMUEL STANLEY

Thomas Hornblower Gill, born in Birmingham, England, 1819, wrote nearly two hundred hymns, and in them he displayed a distinct originality, as well as a deep religious feeling. His New Year's hymn, "Break, new-born year, on glad eyes break," he wrote in 1855 and published it first in his book, *The Golden Chain of Praise Hymns,* 1869. This is one of the most popular of all of his hymns. Besides his volumes of hymns, he wrote *The Fortunes of Faith,* an historical essay on *The Papal Drama,* and a book of memorials of Franklin Howard, entitled *The Triumph of Christ.*

TUNE: Samuel Stanley (1767-1822) was one of the foremost musicians of Birmingham, England, where he was precentor in Carr's Lane Congregational Chapel. In his *Twenty-four Tunes in Four Parts,* about 1796, there first appeared his famous hymn-tune, "Warwick." He was a violoncellist and played in London and in the Birmingham Festivals, 1799, 1802, 1817. In 1828, six years after his death, all of his tunes were published in one volume, which had a large circulation.

224. A Few More Years Shall Roll

TUNE: *"Chalvey"*

HORATIUS BONAR   LEIGHTON G. HAYNE

In his book, *Songs for the Wilderness,* 1844, the Rev. Dr. Horatius Bonar, one of the founders of the Free Church of Scotland, first published his hymn, "A few more years shall roll," which he had written for New Year's Day, 1842. At the time of its composition, he was minister of the North Parish of the Established Church in Kelso. The disruption of that church, in which he had so important a part, did not occur until the following year, 1843. (See No. 115.)

TUNE: The Rev. Dr. Leighton George Hayne (1836-1883), composer of the tune, "Chalvey," was a clergyman in the Church of England. A native of Exeter, he was graduated from Eton and Queen's College, Oxford University. In 1860 the degree of Mus. Doc. was conferred on him.

225. Asleep in Jesus! Blessed Sleep

TUNE: *"Rest"*

MARGARET MACKAY   WILLIAM B. BRADBURY

Margaret Mackay, born in Inverness, Scotland, 1802, was the daughter of Captain Robert Mackay. In 1820 she married Colonel William Mackay, an officer in the English army. She wrote many hymns and poems and also a prose book, *The Family at Heatherdale.* But she is remembered chiefly for her hymn, "Asleep in Jesus! blessed sleep." One day, wandering through the burying-ground of Pennycross Chapel in Devonshire, she read "the simple, but expressive" phrase, "Sleeping in Jesus"; and this led her to write the hymn. Of this experience she has said:

> Distant only a few miles from a bustling and crowded seaport town, reached through a succession of those lovely green lanes for which Devonshire is so remarkable, the quiet aspect of Pennycross comes soothingly over the mind. "Sleeping in Jesus" seems in keeping with it all.

TUNE: "Rest" was composed by William B. Bradbury. (See No. 325.)

226.   Servant of God, Well Done!

TUNE: *"Silver Street"*

CHARLES WESLEY   ISAAC SMITH

Charles Wesley and George Whitefield, great figures in the Wesleyan revival of the eighteenth century, formed a fast friendship when they were both at Oxford University as students; and even in the theological differences over Arminianism and Calvinism, which drove them along different paths, did not destroy that friendship. When Whitefield died, Charles Wesley wrote the hymn, "Servant of God, well done," and entitled it, "An Hymn on the Death of the Rev. George Whitefield." His brother, John Wesley, quoted it at the conclusion of his funeral sermon on Whitefield, delivered on November 18, 1770. This hymn is not to be confused with James Montgomery's hymn of 1816, beginning with the same first line. (See No. 100.)

TUNE: "Silver Street." (See No. 111.)

227.   Rejoice for a Brother Deceased

TUNE: *"Sion"*

CHARLES WESLEY   B. MILGROVE: Harmonized by CHARLES WESLEY

One of Charles Wesley's *Funeral Hymns,* 1744, began with the line, "Rejoice for a brother deceased"; though more timid editors have sometimes printed it, "Weep not for a brother deceased." Wesley was fond of giving out this hymn. Telford tells us that at the conclusion of some of his long horseback journeys, Wesley would at once write down a hymn he had been composing. "When this was done he would look round on those present and salute them with much kindness, ask after their health, give out a short hymn, and thus put all in mind of eternity. He was fond on these occasions of giving out the lines, 'There all the ship's company meet,' " (which is the beginning of the last stanza of this hymn.) (See No. 100.)

TUNE: The tune, "Sion," is often ascribed to B. Milgrove, though this is uncertain. The tune is probably over a hundred and fifty years old. It was used in the Wesleyan revival and is supposed to have been harmonized by Charles Wesley.

228. With Silence Only as Their Benediction

TUNE: *"Benediction"*

JOHN GREENLEAF WHITTIER   ANONYMOUS

The Quaker Poet, John Greenleaf Whittier, in 1845 was deeply saddened by the news of the death of Miss Sophia Sturge, who was the sister of his friend, Joseph Sturge of Birmingham, England. This led him in a spirit of profound sympathy to pen this beautiful hymn on "The good die not." It was published in James Martineau's *Hymns of Praise and Prayer,* 1873. (See No. 2.)

TUNE: The tune, "Benediction," is anonymous.

229. Come, Kingdom of Our God

TUNE: *"St. Thomas"*

JOHN JOHNS   AARON WILLIAMS

The Rev. John Johns, born at Plymouth, England, 1801, became minister of the old Presbyterian chapel, Crediton, 1820, and was appointed in 1836 to be Minister to the Poor at Liverpool. Faithful to his duties, he contracted the fever during an epidemic in the district where he was laboring to relieve the sufferings of the poor, and died on June 23, 1847, a heroic sacrifice to his ideals. His hymn, "Come, kingdom of our God," was headed "Prayer for the Kingdom of God," in Beard's Unitarian *Collection,* in which it was first printed, 1837.

TUNE: "St. Thomas" (See No. 92).

230. The King Shall Come When Morning Dawns

JOHN BROWNLIE   TUNE: *"St. Stephen"*
Based on the Greek   WILLIAM JONES

The Rev. John Brownlie, born in Glasgow, Scotland, 1859, through his *Hymns of the Greek Church,* 1900, attained recognition as a skilled translator of Greek hymns, which was second only to that of Dr. John Mason Neale. His hymn, "The King shall come when morning dawns," is not a direct literal translation, but is based upon an old Greek hymn. He translated hymns also from the Latin and wrote besides ten other original hymns which have come into common use. Julian has said that

"Mr. Brownlie's translations have all the beauty, simplicity, earnestness and elevation of thought and feeling which characterized the originals."

TUNE: The Rev. William Jones (1726-1800), a clergyman of the Church of England, was vicar of Nayland, Suffolk, when in 1789 he composed the tune, "St. Stephen." Two years before this, he preached a memorable sermon on the psalmody of his age, complaining of its lack of regulation. He was a musician of fine skill.

231. The Day of Wrath, That Dreadful Day

WALTER SCOTT   TUNE: *"Irae"*   JOSEPH BARNBY

"Dies irae, dies illa," the thirteenth century Latin hymn, supposed to have been written by a Franciscan Friar, Thomas of Celano, was the most popular hymn in the Middle Ages. Sir Walter Scott's stately translation, which forms our version of the hymn, was used as a climax to Canto 6 in his poem, *The Lay of the Last Minstrel.* Archbishop Trench has said of it:

Nor is it hard to account for its popularity. The metre so grandly devised, of which I remember no other example, fitted though it has here shown itself for bringing out some of the noblest powers of the Latin language—the solemn effect of the triple rhythm, which has been likened to blow following blow of the hammer on the anvil—the confidence of the poet in the universal interest of his theme, a confidence which has made him set out his matter with so majestic and unadorned a plainness as at once to be intelligible to all—these merits, with many more, have given the *Dies Irae* a foremost place among the masterpieces of sacred song.

TUNE: The tune, "Irae," by Sir Joseph Barnby (see No. 14), derives its title from the second word of the Latin hymn, "Dies Irae." The sombre melody with harmony in the minor mode is musically descriptive of the awful emotions aroused by this picture of the final Judgment Day.

232. The Sands of Time Are Sinking

TUNE: *"Rutherford"*

ANNE R. COUSIN   CHRETIAN D'URHAN

"Stand up! stand up for Jesus" was written on the dying words of Dudley Tyng. (See No. 148.) Also the hymn, "The sands of time are sinking," by Anne R. Cousin, is based upon the dying words of "the true saint of the Covenant," Samuel Rutherford (1600-1661), and is blended with some phrases which he wrote during his ministry as a pastor at Anworth and as a professor of theology. Mrs. Cousin (1824-1906) was the wife of a Presbyterian minister. She had found inspiration in the study of the life of the Scotch martyr, Rutherford, and this gave incentive to her for the writing of this hymn. It was first published in *The Christian Treasury,* 1857, and the title of the 1876 edition of her poems was taken from this hymn, *Immanuel's Land and Other Pieces.*

TUNE: Chretian D'Urhan (1788-1845) was born in Montjoie, France, and became a celebrated musician in Paris, identified more with the stage than the church. He was organist, however, for many years in a Jesuit Church in Paris, played the violin with great skill and wrote both vocal and instrumental music. The tune, "Rutherford," was taken from one of his melodies and much altered into a hymn-tune.

233. Thou Art Coming, O My Saviour!

TUNE: *"Beverly"*

FRANCES RIDLEY HAVERGAL   W. H. MONK

Miss Frances Ridley Havergal (1836-1879) wrote her hymn on the Second Coming of Christ, "Thou art coming, O my Saviour," at Winterdyne, England, on November 16, 1873. She also wrote the tune for these words, "St. Paul," but she preferred to have the hymn sung to Doctor Monk's tune, "Beverly." The hymn was printed in a newspaper, *Rock,* in 1873, then in a leaflet, then in her books, *Under the Surface,* 1874, and *Life Mosaic,* 1879. (See No. 110.)

TUNE: William Henry Monk (1823-1889), born in London, England, was a celebrated organist at King's College, Strand, and St. Matthias, Stoke Newington. He was a musical editor of *Hymns Ancient and Modern,* whose title he chose. Twenty-one years after his death, its revised edition contained forty of his tunes.

234. Lo! He Comes with Clouds Descending
Tune: *"Novello"*
Charles Wesley   Samuel Webbe

In *Hymns of Intercession for all Mankind,* 1758, a collection of Wesley hymns, is found the first printing of the hymn, "Lo! He comes with clouds descending," in the form in which it here appears. Other similar hymns are attributed to John Cennick, M. Madan and Matthew Bridges, and many centos have been made on this theme. The Wesley form has been called the English "Dies Irae." It is based on Revelation 1, 7. (See No. 100.)

TUNE: The tune, "Novello," by the organist of the Catholic Sardinian Chapel, London, Samuel Webbe (see No. 84), reminds us through its title that Webbe did much musical editing during his latter years for the London music publishing house of Novello. (See No. 84.)

235. Hark, Hark, My Soul!
Tune: *"Pilgrims"*
Frederick W. Faber   Henry Smart

"The Pilgrims of the Night" is the title which Father Frederick W. Faber, a Roman Catholic priest (formerly of the Church of England), gave to his tender hymn of heaven, "Hark, hark, my soul!" It was first published in his *Oratory Hymn Book* in 1854, and has since been widely adopted by Protestants and Catholics alike, at first largely through its introduction into the Appendix of *Hymns Ancient and Modern,* 1868. (See No. 38.)

TUNE: Henry Smart wrote the tune, "Pilgrims," for the Appendix to *Hymns Ancient and Modern,* 1868, wherein it was first published. Its title is derived from one word in the title of the hymn by Faber, "Pilgrims of the Night." (See No. 7.)

236. The Homeland! O the Homeland!
Tune: *"Homeland"*
Hugh R. Haweis   Arthur S. Sullivan

The Rev. Hugh R. Haweis (1838-1901), son of Canon J. W. O. Haweis of Chichester, England, was a clergyman in the Church of England, a skilled musician and choir-master, a writer of many books, and magazine editor, and (if an unsupported tradition be true) the author of the much-loved hymn, "The Homeland! O the Homeland!" The last church to which he ministered was St. James's, Marylebone, London.

TUNE: "The Homeland" was Sir Arthur S. Sullivan's first hymn-tune. It was set to the hymn, attributed to Hugh R. Haweis, from which it derives its title, and was published in *Good Words,* 1867. (See No. 73.)

237. "Forever with the Lord!"

TUNE: *"Vigil"*

JAMES MONTGOMERY

GIOVANNI PAISIELLO

"At Home in Heaven" is the winsome title which James Montgomery, the militant editor in Sheffield, England, gave to his hymn, "Forever with the Lord." It saw the light in his book, *A Poet's Portfolio,* London, 1835. Two of the omitted stanzas are worth quoting:

> Yet clouds will intervene,
>   And all my prospect flies;
> Like Noah's dove, I flit between
>   Rough seas and stormy skies.

> Anon the clouds depart,
>   The winds and waters cease,
> While sweetly o'er my gladdened heart
>   Expands the bow of peace.

(See No. 51.)

TUNE: Giovanni Paisiello, composer of the music from which the hymn-tune, "Vigil," has been taken, was an Italian composer, who was born in 1741, and died in 1816.

238. One Sweetly Solemn Thought

TUNE: *"Dulce Domum"*

PHOEBE CARY

R. S. AMBROSE

The Congregational Quarterly of October, 1874, states that Phoebe Cary's hymn, "One sweetly solemn thought," was written (as she herself has told) in the little, back, third-story bedroom, one Sabbath morning in 1852, on her return from church. She and her sister, Alice Cary, both of them poets who afterwards won distinction, were then living humbly in New York city, having come from their home in the suburbs of Cincinnati, that same year. Though not written as a hymn, it was published as such in the Protestant Episcopal *Hymns for Church and Home,* 1860; and in England it became popularized through the Moody and Sankey evangelistic campaign.

TUNE: "Dulce Domum," a title derived from the Latin words, meaning "Sweet Home," is a hymn-tune which has been arranged from a vocal solo by R. S. Ambrose of Hamilton, Ontario, set to the original poem by Phoebe Cary, "One sweetly solemn thought."

239. O Paradise! O Paradise

TUNE: *"Paradise"*

FREDERICK W. FABER   HENRY SMART

Under the title, "Paradise," Father Frederick W. Faber first published his hymn, "O Paradise! O Paradise!" in his *Hymns,* 1862. When it appeared in *Hymns Ancient and Modern,* the last stanza of the hymn, "Lord Jesus, King of Paradise," was written by the editors of that hymnal and added to the hymn in order to reach a better climax. (See No. 38.)

TUNE: "Paradise," the hymn-tune by the blind English organist, Henry Smart, takes its title from Father Faber's hymn, for which it was composed. (See No. 7.)

240. Ten Thousand Times Ten Thousand

TUNE: *"Alford"*

HENRY ALFORD   JOHN B. DYKES

Dean Henry Alford of Canterbury (1810-1871), who was recognized as a great biblical scholar and an eloquent preacher, wrote this joyous hymn of heaven in 1867, and published it first in his book, *Year of Praise,* that same year. When he died in 1871, this hymn was sung at his funeral in Canterbury, and as if to memorialize the heavenward look which the hymn expresses and which was characteristic of his life, this epitaph was placed upon his tomb, "Deversorium victoris proficientis Hierosolymam" ("The inn of a pilgrim traveling to Jerusalem").

TUNE: "Alford" (See Nos. 200 and 113).

241. Jerusalem the Golden

TUNE: *"Ewing"*

BERNARD OF CLUNY
Translated by JOHN M. NEALE

ALEXANDER EWING

Bernard of Morlaix, or of Cluny, a devout monk of the twelfth century, entered the Abbey of Cluny when Peter the Venerable was at its head. Profoundly stirred by the wickedness and vices of the world around him, he composed his famous poem, *De Contemptu Mundi,* as a protest against the sins of his age. From that portion of the long Latin poem, wherein he looks away from the evil world to the pure and golden splendors of heaven, are taken the lines, beginning, "Urbs Syon aurea, patria lactea, cive decora," which Dr. John M. Neale has translated into our hymn, "Jerusalem the golden." Doctor Neale published the section of the poem, of which this is a part in *The Rhythm of Bernard of Morlaix, Monk of Cluny, or the Celestial Country,* 1858. Dr. Philip Schaff calls this "the sweetest of all the New Jerusalem hymns of heavenly homesickness which have taken their inspiration from the last two chapters of Revelation." (See No. 108.)

TUNE: The tune, "Ewing," originally set to "For thee, O dear, dear country," takes its name from its composer, Alexander Ewing (1830-1895), a native of Aberdeen, Scotland, educated as a lawyer, and an amateur player on different instruments. One night at a rehearsal of The Harmonic Choir, one of its members, Ewing, showed a 3/2 hymn-tune of his own composition to the leader, William Carnie, with the request that the choir sing it, which they did. It was printed on slips in 1853, and later, changed to common time, was printed in *Hymns Ancient and Modern* as "Ewing." The composer never liked the change, saying, "It now seems to me a good deal like a polka." After serving with the British Army in the Crimea, and with General Gordon in China, he returned to Taunton, and died there in 1895.

242. Rise, My Soul, and Stretch Thy Wings

TUNE: *"Amsterdam"*

ROBERT SEAGRAVE   JAMES NARES

The Rev. Robert Seagrave, English Calvinistic Methodist (1693-1756), wrote fifty original hymns which were published in his own hymnal, *Hymns for Christian Worship, Partly Composed and Partly Collected from Various Authors,* 1742. Among them was "Rise, my soul, and stretch thy wings," which has proved to be his most popular hymn. It was entitled, "The Pilgrim's Song."

TUNE: Dr. James Nares (1715-1783), born in Stanwell, England, was organist in York Cathedral, 1734, and the Royal Chapel, London, 1756. Cambridge University granted him the degree of Mus. Doc. in 1756. He composed the hymn-tune, "Amsterdam," among many other hymn-tunes and anthems. It was published in the *Foundry Collection,* 1742.

243. There Is a Land of Pure Delight

TUNE: *"Varina"*

ISAAC WATTS   GEORGE F. ROOT

"A Prospect of Heaven Makes Death Easy," as Dr. Isaac Watts entitled his hymn, "There is a land of pure delight," was written in Southampton on the south coast of England. The second stanza:

Sweet fields beyond the swelling flood
Stand dressed in living green,

was suggested to his mind by the vision one gets near Southampton of the green fields of the Isle of Wight, "beyond the swelling flood," of the strait that flows between the island and the main land of England. It was first published in Watts's *Hymns and Spiritual Songs,* 1707. (See No. 174.)

TUNE: "Varina" was a hymn-tune composed by the American song-writer, George Frederick Root. (See No. 288.)

244. O Mother Dear, Jerusalem

TUNE: *"Materna"*

AUTHOR UNKNOWN

SAMUEL A. WARD

Hymnology has never determined who was "F. B. P.," whose initials are attached to the original manuscript of the hymn, "O mother dear, Jerusalem." It is now in the British Museum, London.

TUNE: "Materna" (See No. 145).

245. Christian, Dost Thou See Them

TUNE: *"St. Andrew of Crete"*

ANDREW OF CRETE
Translated by JOHN M. NEALE

JOHN B. DYKES

Archbishop Andrew of Crete (660-732) was born in Damascus, lived for years in a monastery at Jerusalem, and spent the latter part of his life in the archbishopric at Crete. He was famed as the author of "The Great Canon." From *Stichera for the Second Week of the Great Fast,* Dr. John Mason Neale's translation from Andrew, is taken our hymn, "Christian, dost thou see them?" The title gives us the clue that Andrew wrote these lines for use during the Lenten season. Cast in the form of question and answer, the hymn is a dramatic presentation of the temptations from fear (stanza 1), allurement of sin (2), discouragement (3), and weariness (4), which beset the militant Christian. (See No. 108.)

TUNE: The tune by Dr. John B. Dykes, "St. Andrew of Crete," was so named after the author of the hymn, for which it was composed. (See No. 113.)

246. Watchman, Tell Us of the Night

Tune: *"Watchman"*

John Bowring   Lowell Mason

Another hymn in the form of question and answer is Sir John Bowring's missionary song, "Watchman, tell us of the night," based on Isaiah 21, 11, and first published in his *Hymns,* 1825. Dr. Charles S. Robinson has written of the scene the hymn described, as follows:

The scene is laid in the midst of the Babylonish captivity. A lonely watchman is represented as standing on the ramparts of some tower along the defenses of the citadel. He seems to be anxiously looking for the issues of the siege leveled against it. The time is midnight. Calamity is over the land. . . . Suddenly an unknown voice pierces the air, whether in wailing sorrow or in bitter taunt, is not evident; but out of the stillness already grown oppressive breaks the question with repetitious pertinacity: "Watchman, what of the night? Watchman, what of the night?" The sentinel waits through a moment of surprised meditation, and then tranquilly answers: "The morning cometh and also the night: if ye will inquire, inquire ye: return, come."

TUNE: "Watchman" takes its title from Sir John Bowring's hymn for which it was composed by Lowell Mason in 1830. (See No. 21.)

247. In Christ There Is No East or West

Tune: *"St. Peter's Oxford"*

John Oxenham   Alexander R. Reinagle

John Oxenham, author of "In Christ there is no east or west," is an English poet and novelist. He was educated at Old Trafford School and Victoria University, Manchester. Entering business, he lived for a while in France and in this country. For a time he contemplated orange-growing in the south. But on his return to England he dropped business and devoted his time to writing. Fifty-five publications, of poetry and prose, are credited to him. In 1925 his wife, who before their marriage was Miss Margery Anderson, died, leaving him two sons and four daughters. He is an expert Alpine climber. He has written many excellent hymns, the most popular of which in this country is this modern missionary hymn.

TUNE: Alexander Robert Reinagle (1799-1877), born at Brighton, England, was once organist in St. Peter's-in-the-East Church at Oxford: hence the title of the tune. He was the nephew of Alexander Reinagle, a violinist who played for John Wesley.

248. Christ for the World We Sing

TUNE: *"Italian Hymn"*

SAMUEL WOLCOTT

FELICE DE GIARDINI

The Rev. Dr. Samuel Wolcott, born in South Windham, Connecticut, was serving a pastorate in Cleveland, Ohio, when he wrote the hymn, "Christ for the world we sing," of which he gave the following account:

The Young Men's Christian Association of Ohio met in one of our churches with their motto in evergreen letters over the pulpit: "Christ for the world, the world for Christ." This suggested the hymn, "Christ for the world we sing." It was on my way home from this service in 1869, walking alone through the streets, that I put together the four stanzas of the hymn.

Before his pastorates in Providence, Rhode Island, Chicago, and Cleveland, he was a missionary in Syria (1841-2), and afterwards was secretary of the Ohio Home Missionary Society.

TUNE: "Italian Hymn." (See No. 9.)

249. Saviour, Sprinkle Many Nations

TUNE: *"Weston"*

ARTHUR CLEVELAND COXE

J. E. ROE

Bishop Arthur Cleveland Coxe (1818-1896) before his elevation to the episcopacy was rector of St. John's Protestant Episcopal Church in Hartford, Connecticut. Here on Good Friday of 1850 he began the writing of his hymn, "Saviour, sprinkle many nations," and completed it the following year in the grounds of Magdelen College, Oxford, while on a summer visit to England. It was published in England by the Rev. Ernest Hawkins, that same year, in his *Verses for 1851, in Commemoration of the Third Jubilee of the Society for the Propagation of the*

Gospel. The only reason it did not appear in the *Protestant Episcopal Hymnal,* prepared by the Hymnal Commission of 1869-71, of which Bishop Coxe was a member, was the veto of the author against its use in that hymnal. (See No. 91.)

TUNE: John Edward Roe, an English composer, who wrote the tune "Weston," was born in 1831, and died in 1871.

250. Hail to the Lord's Anointed

TUNE: *"Lymington"*

James Montgomery   R. Jackson

James Montgomery wrote his hymn, "Hail to the Lord's Anointed," for a Christmas meeting in one of the Moravian Settlements in England, 1821. Dr. Adam Clarke, presiding at a Wesleyan missionary meeting in Liverpool, April 14, 1822, heard the author quote this hymn in an address, and made this statement regarding it in his *Commentary:*

> The following poetical version of some of the principal passages of the foregoing Psalm was made and kindly given to me by my much-respected friend, James Montgomery, Esq., of Sheffield. I need not tell the intelligent reader that he has seized the spirit and exhibited some of the principal beauties of the Hebrew bard, though, to use his own words in a letter to me, his "hand trembled to touch the harp of Zion." I take the liberty here to register a wish, which I have strongly expressed to himself, that he would favor the Church of God with a metrical version of the whole book.

(See No. 51.)

TUNE: The tune, "Lymington," is attributed to R. Jackson; though it is not certain just who he is (possibly the famous tenor singer, born in 1879).

251. Jesus Shall Reign Where'er the Sun

TUNE: *"Duke Street"*

Isaac Watts   John Hatton

"Jesus shall reign where'er the sun" does not sound like a translation from the psalms; but Dr. Isaac Watts in his effort to Christianize "the language of David" made this translation of a part of Psalm 72. In Watts's poem the second and third stanzas (out of which our second stanza was made) show that Watts added some modern geography to the psalm:

> Behold the islands with their kings,
> And Europe, her best tribute brings;
> From north to south the princes meet
> To pay their homage at his feet.
>
> There Persia, glorious to behold,
> There India shines in Eastern gold,
> And barbarous nations at his word
> Submit and bow, and own their Lord.

"Christ's Kingdom Among the Gentiles" was Watts's title for the hymn, when it was first published, 1719, in *The Psalms of David Imitated in the Language of the New Testament.* (See No. 174.)

TUNE: John Hatton, who wrote "Duke Street," was an English composer, born in Warrenton, near Liverpool, and died in 1793, at Saint Helens, Windle. The tune is named for Duke Street, where he lived, and was published in Henry Boyd's *A Select Collection of Psalms and Hymn Tunes,* Glascow, 1793, where it is entitled "Addison's Nineteenth Psalm."

252. Fling Out the Banner! Let It Float

TUNE: *"Doane"*

GEORGE W. DOANE

JOHN B. CALKIN

When the girls of St. Mary's School, Burlington, New Jersey, in 1848, were planning to raise a new flag, they asked the Founder of the School, their beloved Bishop George Washington Doane, to write a new hymn for the occasion. His missionary lines, beginning, "Fling out the banner," were the result. Under the title, "The Banner of the Cross," it was published in *Songs by the Way,* 1875. (See No. 29.)

TUNE: The tune, "Doane," by John Baptiste Calkin (see No. 74), was named for Bishop Doane, author of the hymn to which it is here set.

253. The Morning Light Is Breaking

SAMUEL F. SMITH   TUNE: *"Webb"*   G. J. WEBB

The author of "My Country, 'tis of thee," the Rev. Dr. Samuel F. Smith, wrote his hymn, "The morning light is breaking," in 1832, the year when he was graduated from Andover Theological Seminary. It was published, 1832, in Thomas Hastings's *Spiritual Songs.* Doctor Smith wrote of this hymn:

It has been a great favorite at missionary gatherings, and I have myself heard it sung in five or six different languages in Europe and Asia. It is a favorite with the Burmans, Karens and Telegus in Asia, from whose lips I heard it repeated.

TUNE: "Webb" (See No. 148).

254. The Day Thou Gavest, Lord, Is Ended

TUNE: *"St. Clement"*

JOHN ELLERTON   CLEMENT C. SCHOLEFIELD

The Rev. John Ellerton's hymn, "The day Thou gavest," was written in 1870 for a Liturgy for Missionary Meetings, and later was revised for *Church Hymns,* the next year. Julian has said of his hymns: "His sympathy with nature, especially in her sadder moods, is great; he loves the fading light and the peace of eve." (See No. 33.)

TUNE: The Rev. Clement Cotterill Scholefield (1839-1904) was graduated from Cambridge University and entered the ministry of the Church of England, 1867. He served as vicar of St. Trinity, Kingsbridge. The title of his tune, "St. Clement," gives evidence that some hymnal editor desired to canonize the priestly composer.

255. Wake the Song of Jubilee

TUNE: *"Advent Garrett"*

LEONARD BACON   GEORGE M. GARRETT

The Rev. Dr. Leonard Bacon (1802-1881) was graduated from Yale College and Andover Theological Seminary. While he was a student at Andover he published a small collection, *Hymns and Sacred Songs for the Monthly Concert* (for missions), 1823, and this contained his hymn, "Wake the song of jubilee." Somewhat altered, it appeared in Pratt's *Psalms and Hymns,* London, 1829. The author accepted the alterations as improvements, and this hymn, a product of his student days, has become widely accepted as a rousing missionary hymn.

TUNE: Dr. George Mursell Garrett, born in England, 1834, was organist at Cambridge University, and from that ancient institution he received his musical doctorate. His tune, originally entitled, "Advent," is called "Advent Garrett," to distinguish it from another "Advent" tune by Berthold Tours.

256. O Zion, Haste

TUNE: *"Tidings"*

MARY A. THOMSON   JAMES WALCH

Mrs. Mary Ann Thomson, born in London, England, was wife of the librarian of the Free Library, Philadelphia, and she has told this remarkable story of the writing of her famous missionary hymn:

> I wrote the greater part of the hymn, "O Zion, haste," in the year 1868. I had written many hymns before, and one night, while I was sitting up with one of my children who was ill of typhoid fever, I thought I should like to write a missionary hymn to the tune of the hymn beginning, "Hark, hark, my soul, angelic songs are swelling," as I was fond of that tune; but as I could not then get a refrain I liked, I left the hymn unfinished and about three years later I finished it by writing the refrain which now forms part of it.

Tune: James Walch, who was born in England, 1837, was a well-known organist and composer of church music. His best-known hymn-tune is "Tidings."

257. O Happy Home Where Thou Art Loved

TUNE: *"Alverstroke"*

CARL J. P. SPITTA   JOSEPH BARNBY

The Rev. Carl Johann Philipp Spitta, born in Hanover, Germany, 1801, began his career as a watch-maker, but later studied theology and became a Lutheran pastor, serving many churches until his death in 1859. He wrote many hymns, one of which has been translated by Mrs. Alexander into our lines, beginning, "O happy home, where Thou art loved the dearest."

Tune: Sir Joseph Barnby (see No. 14) was the composer of this joyful tune, "Alverstroke," set to Spitta's hymn on the happy home.

258. On This Stone Now Laid with Prayer

TUNE: *"Pleyel's Hymn"*

JOHN PIERPONT   IGNACE J. PLEYEL

The Rev. John Pierpont, grandfather of the late John Pierpont Morgan, was a prominent Unitarian pastor in Boston for many years, though his hymn, "On this stone now laid with prayer," has a distinct Trinitarian form; the first stanza, mentioning the Lord; the second, Jesus Christ; the third, the Spirit. The Suffolk Street Chapel in Boston was about to be started and Pierpont was asked to write a hymn for the corner-stone laying on May 23, 1839. This hymn, as the result of the request, was sung on that occasion, and was published in the author's *Airs of Palestine and Other Poems,* 1840. The line, "For the outcast and the poor," describes the special mission for which the Suffolk Street Chapel was intended.

TUNE: The tune, "Pleyel's Hymn," was named for its composer, Ignace J. Pleyel (see No. 165), and is his best-known melody today. In English hymnals it is called "German Hymn," mistakenly, for Pleyel was an Austrian. The melody is derived from the slow movement of the quartet, No. 4, Opus 7, by Pleyel—an andante with variations.

259. Christ Is Made the Sure Foundation

TUNE: *"Regent Square"*

From the Latin   HENRY SMART
Translated by JOHN M. NEALE

The author of the Latin hymn of the sixth century, "Urbs beata Hierusalem," has never been determined. Dr. John Mason Neale, however, has made this stately hymn on the church available for our use through his excellent translation, beginning, "Christ is made the sure Foundation." As he published it in his *Mediaeval Hymns,* 1851, it contained nine stanzas. (See No. 108.)

TUNE: "Regent Square." (See No. 7.)

260. Revive Thy Work, O Lord
Tune: *"Swabia"*

Albert Midlane   Johann M. Spiess

Albert Midlane (1825-1909), who was born at Newport on the Isle of Wight, ascribed to his Sunday school teacher his first inspiration to write hymns, and as a result he penned hundreds of hymns nearly one hundred of which have passed into common use. His hymn, "Revive Thy work, O Lord," was first published in *The British Messenger* in October, 1858. The second line of stanza five was originally, "Give pentecostal showers."

TUNE: Johann Martin Spiess was born in Honsolgen, Swabia, August 24, 1683. He published many solos with stringed obligato, motets, sonatas for strings, masses and requiems. His *Cithera Davidis* was a collection of vesper psalms. He was Prior of Yrsee Monastery when he died, July 2, 1761. His hymn-tune, "Swabia," is named for his birth-place.

261. By Cool Siloam's Shady Rill
Tune: *"Siloam"*

Reginald Heber   Isaac B. Woodbury

"Christ a Pattern for Children" was the title of Bishop Reginald Heber's hymn, "By cool Siloam's shady rill," when it was first published in the English *Christian Observer,* 1812. He was then the Vicar of Hodnet, England, and not until eleven years later was he elected Bishop of Calcutta. Afterwards he rewrote the hymn, and his wife included it in the posthumous collection of his hymns. It is based on Luke 2, 40: "And the child grew, and waxed strong in spirit, filled with wisdom; and the grace of God was upon him."

TUNE: Isaac Baker Woodbury (1819-1858), a native of Beverly, Massachusetts, became a blacksmith and then a vocal teacher and composer. He wrote his tune, "Siloam," on board a ship that was being tossed by a storm at sea. It was published in the *Boston Musical Education Society Collection of Church Music,* 1842. It derives its title from the first line of the hymn.

262.   There's a Friend for Little Children

TUNE: *"Edengrove"*

ALBERT MIDLANE   SAMUEL SMITH

Arthur Midlane wrote his hymn, "There's a Friend for little children," on February 27, 1859, and it was published in December of that year in *Good News for the Little Ones.* The stanzas have since been rearranged into a different and better sequence: the original contained six stanzas and was entitled, "Jesus, the Children's Friend." (See No. 260.)

TUNE: Samuel Smith, composer of the tune, "Edengrove," or "Eden Grove," as it is sometimes given, was organist of the parish church in Windsor, England. In 1865 he published a small collection of his own hymn-tunes, in which "Eden Grove" appeared for the first time.

263.   Brightly Gleams Our Banner

TUNE: *"St. Theresa"*

THOMAS J. POTTER   ARTHUR S. SULLIVAN

The Rev. Thomas J. Potter (1827-1873) was born in Scarborough, England, and became a Roman Catholic priest. For years he was professor of Pulpit Eloquence and English Literature in the Foreign Missionary College of All Hallows, Dublin, Ireland, in which city he died. His hymn, "Brightly gleams our banner," is thoroughly Roman in its original form (popular among Catholic schools today); but the phrases and stanzas, objectionable to Protestant doctrine, have been eliminated for our worship. It first appeared in *The Holy Family Hymns,* 1860.

TUNE: The tune, "St. Theresa," was written by Sir Arthur S. Sullivan in 1874.   (See No. 73.)

264.   I Think When I Read that Sweet Story

TUNE: *"Sweet Story"*

JEMIMA LUKE   English Melody

Mrs. Jemima Luke, the daughter of Thomas Thompson, was a native of Colebrooke Terrace, Islington, England, and in 1843 at the age of twenty married the Rev. Samuel

Luke, a Congregational minister. Julian tells us the story of its composition:

It is recorded that this hymn was composed in a stage coach in 1841, and was designed for use in the village school, near her father's seat, Poundsford Park. It was published anonymously in the *Leeds Hymn Book*, 1853.

TUNE: "Sweet Story" is an old English traditional melody of unknown origin.

265. Hushed Was the Evening Hymn

TUNE: *"Samuel"*

JAMES D. BURNS   ARTHUR S. SULLIVAN

The Rev. James Drummond Burns, a native of Edinburgh (1823) was a minister, first in the Free Church, and later in the Presbyterian Church, in which he served a parish in London until his death (1864). His charming hymn on the Child Samuel, "Hushed was the evening hymn," was first published in his small book of prayers and hymns for each evening of a month, *Evening Hymns,* 1857.

TUNE: The tune, "Samuel," composed by Sir Arthur S. Sullivan in 1874, takes its title from the central figure in Burns's hymn. (See No. 73.)

266. Almighty Lord, with One Accord

TUNE: *"Amazon"*

M. WOOLSEY STRYKER   Arranged from CARL G. GLAESER
                                              By LOWELL MASON

President Melancthon Woolsey Stryker, a Presbyterian clergyman from the time of his graduation from Auburn Theological Seminary, 1876, after serving in several pastorates, was made the president of Hamilton College, his old Alma Mater, in 1892. Four years later he wrote for the students at Hamilton "A College Hymn," beginning, "Almighty Lord, with one accord." It is a hymn for youth, and a prayer that education may be blended with religion.

TUNE: "Azmon" (See Nos. 8 and 21).

267. Shepherd of Tender Youth

TUNE: *"Dort"*

CLEMENT OF ALEXANDRIA
Translated by HENRY M. DEXTER

LOWELL MASON

The oldest Christian hymn of the church, whose date of authorship can be approximated (200 A. D.), is a Greek hymn by the famous theologian of Alexandria, Titus Flavius Clemens, or Saint Clement. The first line, literally translated, is "Tamer of unbridled steeds." The Rev. Dr. Henry M. Dexter, a Congregational clergyman, translated it from the Greek in 1848, four years after his graduation from Andover Theological Seminary, and thus made our lovely hymn, "Shepherd of tender youth," and published it, the following year, in the *Congregationalist.*

TUNE: The tune, "Dort," was composed by Lowell Mason in 1832. (See No. 21.)

268. The Lord Our God Alone is Strong

TUNE: *"Melcombe"*

CALEB T. WINCHESTER

SAMUEL WEBBE

Professor Caleb T. Winchester wrote his hymn, "The Lord our God alone is strong," as a dedication hymn for the Orange Judd Hall of Natural Science, Wesleyan University, in Middletown, Connecticut, on July 17, 1871. He was at the time librarian of the college, and later became distinguished as the professor of English Literature in the same institution and as an authoritative critic and lecturer.

TUNE: "Melcombe" (See No. 84).

269. Father, Who on Man Dost Shower

TUNE: *"Quem Pastores Laudavere"*

PERCY DEARMER

15th Century German Melody

The Rev. Dr. Percy Dearmer, professor of Ecclesiastical Art in King's College, London, and stationed at Holy Trinity Church, Sloane Street, is one of England's foremost living hymnists. Born in London, February 27, 1867, the son of an artist, Thomas Dearmer, he was educated at Westminster School, and Christ Church, Oxford. He has ministered in many churches, acted as secretary to the London Branch of the Christian Social Union, and in 1915 served as chaplain to the British Red Cross in Servia, for which he received a decoration. In 1916 he helped the Y. M. C. A. in France, later joining the Mission of Help in India, 1916-1917. He lectured in Delhi during the next year, and visited Japan and America, 1918-19. Among the thirty-six books he has written or edited are *The English Liturgy,* 1903, *The English Carol Book,* 1913 and (second series) 1919, *The Art of Public Worship,* 1919, and *Songs of Praise,* 1925, one of England's greatest hymn collections. In 1906 he was an editor of the *English Hymnal,* 1906. His hymns are among the best of his generation, and his hymn, "Father, who on man dost shower," is one of his finest.

TUNE: "Quem Pastores Laudavere," a fifteenth century German tune, is well suited to the dignity of Doctor Dearmer's hymn.

270. O Thou, Before Whose Presence
TUNE: *"Hodges"*
SAMUEL J. STONE   JOHN S. B. HODGES

The temperance hymn, "O Thou, before whose presence," by the Rev. Samuel John Stone was contributed by him to the 1889 *Supplemental Hymns* to the *Hymns Ancient and Modern.* Stone was born at Whitmore, Staffordshire, England, 1839, was graduated from Pembroke College, Oxford, 1862, and after entering the ministry served many parishes in the Church of England. He wrote many books of poetry. He died in 1900.

TUNE: The tune, "Hodges," has taken its title from the last name of its composer, John S. B. Hodges. (See No. 98.)

271. Eternal Father, Strong to Save
TUNE: *"Melita"*
WILLIAM WHITING   JOHN B. DYKES

William Whiting (1825-1878) was the Master of the Winchester College Choristers' School in England. Although he wrote a number of hymns, only one has survived in common use, his hymn, written in 1860 for those at sea, "Eternal Father, strong to save." The paucity of good hymns on the subject has contributed to its popularity. Whiting made a Latin version of the hymn; and Hodges of Frome wrote a story, based on it, entitled "Hymn 222."

TUNE: "Melita" (See Nos. 63 and 113).

272. O Beautiful for Spacious Skies

TUNE: *"Materna"*

KATHARINE LEE BATES   SAMUEL A. WARD

Standing on the summit of Pike's Peak in Colorado, after a visit to the Columbian Exposition in Chicago, in the summer of 1893, Miss Katharine Lee Bates, professor of English Literature in Wellesley College, was so filled with the sense of the greatness of her country and so thrilled with the spirit of patriotism, that she was stirred to write her hymn, "O beautiful for spacious skies." Her phrases "amber waves of grain" and "purple mountain majesties above the fruited plain," are derived from the scene she there witnessed; but her prayers to God to "crown thy good with brotherhood" came from her yearning for America to become a righteous nation, filled with the Christian spirit and unified with true brotherhood.

TUNE: "Materna" (See No. 145).

273. O Beautiful, My Country!

TUNE: *"Lancashire"*

FREDERICK L. HOSMER   HENRY SMART

The Rev. Dr. Frederick L. Hosmer, born in 1840, was a native of Framingham, Massachusetts, and died in Berkeley, California, in June, 1930. He was graduated from Harvard University in 1862, and entering the Unitarian ministry, he served churches in New England, Cleveland, Ohio, St. Louis, Missouri, and Berkeley, California. He was a prolific writer of hymns, usually marked by rare literary beauty and spiritual power. His patriotic hymn, "O beautiful, my country" is growing in popularity. He edited *Unity Hymns,* 1880, and wrote *The Way of*

Life, 1877, *The Thought of God in Hymns and Poems,* 1885, and (second series) 1894.

TUNE: "Lancashire" (See Nos. 7 and 138).

274. Lord of Earth, Thy Forming Hand

TUNE: *"Maidstone"*

ROBERT GRANT

WILLIAM B. GILBERT

Sir Robert Grant (1785-1838) wrote his hymn, "Lord of earth, Thy forming hand," while he was Governor of Bombay. It appeared, 1835, in H. V. Elliott's *Psalms and Hymns for Public, Private and Social Worship,* a book which "had a marked influence upon later hymn-books," according to Julian, and the year after Sir Robert's death in his *Sacred Poems,* which his brother, Lord Glenelg, published in his memory (1839). It is based on Psalm 73, 25. (See No. 1.)

TUNE: Walter B. Gilbert was born in Exeter, England, in 1829, and died in 1910. He was a musical editor and composed much church music, including the hymn-tune, "Maidstone."

275. God of Our Fathers, Whose Almighty Hand

TUNE: *"National Hymn"*

DANIEL C. ROBERTS

GEORGE W. WARREN

The Rev. Daniel C. Roberts (1841-1907), a member of the Ohio Volunteers, 84th Regiment, during the Civil War, was asked by the citizens of Brandon, Vermont, where he was serving as the Protestant Episcopal rector, to write a hymn for the centenary of the American Republic, July 4, 1876. The request produced this hymn, "God of our fathers, whose almighty hand," which was sung on that patriotic occasion in Brandon, and since then throughout the country.

TUNE: Roberts's hymn, "God of our fathers," was originally sung to the tune, "Russian Hymn," by Alexis T. Lwoff (see No. 279); but later George William Warren (1828-1902), organist in St. Peter's Church, Albany, New York, and then in the Church of the Holy Trinity, Brooklyn, composed the tune, "National Hymn," especially for these words.

276. My Country, 'Tis of Thee

TUNE: *"America"*

SAMUEL F. SMITH   HENRY CAREY

The Rev. Dr. Samuel Francis Smith (1808-1895) has left us the following story of the writing of his patriotic hymn, "My Country, 'tis of thee":

This song was written in 1832. I found the tune in a German music book brought to this country by the late William C. Woodbridge and put into my hands by Lowell Mason, Esq., because, he said, I could read German books and he could not. It is not, however, a translation, but the expression of my thought at the moment of glancing at the tune.

Born in Boston, 1808, he was graduated from Harvard and Andover Theological Seminary, entered the Baptist ministry and served as editor of the Baptist Missionary Union publications. He was co-editor of *The Psalmist,* a Baptist hymnal, and published also *Lyric Gems,* 1854, and *Rock of Ages,* 1870. He died in 1895.

TUNE: Henry Carey, if indeed he was the composer of the tune, called "America" (many doubt it), was born in England, 1685, and died, 1743. Between those dates he wrote cantatas and poems and nine ballad-operas. This tune is used to "God, save the King," the English national hymn, and its title, "America," in American hymnals is little short of humorous.

277. God Bless Our Native Land

TUNE: *"America"*

CHARLES T. BROOKS and JOHN S. DWIGHT   HENRY CAREY

Two Harvard students of '35 and '36 collaborated in writing the patriotic hymn, "God bless our native land." They both afterwards became clergymen, the Rev. Charles T. Brooks and the Rev. John S. Dwight. Brooks founded his poem on a German hymn, "Gott senge Sachsenland," and later Dwight made some alterations. Lowell Mason then published it in 1844.

TUNE: "America" (See No. 276).

278. We Plow the Fields and Scatter

TUNE: *"Dresden"*

MATTHIAS CLAUDIUS
Translated by JANE M. CAMPBELL

JOHANN A. P. SCHULZ

Matthias Claudius (1740-1815) was a much-loved German poet, the son of a clergyman. He wrote in 1782 a short drama, *Paul Erdmann's Fest,* in which occurred a scene where the peasants at harvest time bring in the fruits of the fields, and then sing the Peasants' Song, "Wir pflügen und wir streuen." From this Miss Jane Montgomery Campbell translated the thanksgiving hymn, "We plow the fields and scatter." It was published under the title, "Thanksgiving for the Harvest," in C. S. Bere's *Garland of Songs,* 1861.

TUNE: The tune, "Dresden," is taken from the work of Johann Abraham Peter Schulz, who was born in Lüneburg, March 31, 1747, and died in Schweldt, January 10, 1800. He was a music director in Berlin and later chapel-master to the King of Denmark in Copenhagen, 1787. While he composed a number of operas, oratorios, hymn-tunes and instrumental music, he is remembered in Germany mostly for his songs.

279. God, the All-Terrible

TUNE: *"Russian Hymn"*

HENRY T. CHORLEY

ALEXIS T. LWOFF

Henry F. Chorley wrote his hymn of peace, "God the All-Terrible," to the melody of the Russian national hymn, and it was printed in 1842 in Hullah's *Part Music.* During the Franco-German War on August 28, 1870, the Rev. John Ellerton wrote "God, the Almighty One, wisely ordaining," in imitation of Chorley's lines. These two hymns have sometimes been blended into a cento in some of the hymnals, such as *Church Hymns,* 1871.

TUNE: "Russian Hymn" was the tune, composed in 1833, for the national hymn of Russia by Joulowsky during the Czaristic regime. It is anathema today in the land of the Soviet. Its composer, Alexis T. Lwoff, was a distinguished Russian musician, who was born in 1799 and died in 1870. He wrote the tune one night very late on his return home, and soon afterward it was given before the Czar and Czarina in the Court Chapel by a choir and orchestra. It made so fine an impression that it was formally decreed on December 4, 1833, to be the official army hymn.

280. Not Alone for Mighty Empire

TUNE: *"Austrian Hymn"*

WILLIAM P. MERRILL   FRANZ J. HAYDN

The Rev. Dr. William P. Merrill, then pastor of the Sixth Presbyterian Church, Chicago, on Thanksgiving Day, 1908, wrote his hymn, "Not alone for mighty empire," on his return from a Union Thanksgiving Service in the Forty-first Street Presbyterian Church of that city, especially inspired by a prayer offered at that service by the Rev. Jenkin Lloyd Jones. Doctor Merrill, born in Orange, New Jersey, 1867, and graduated from Rutgers College, 1887, and Union Theological Seminary, 1890, has served Presbyterian churches in Philadelphia, Chicago and New York city, where he is now pastor of the famous Brick Presbyterian Church. He is author of eight books and president of the trustees of the Church Peace Union. His hymns, with a strong social service flavor, are meeting a widening popularity.

TUNE: "Austrian Hymn" (See Nos. 90 and 17).

281. Sing to the Lord of Harvest

TUNE: *"Greenland"*

JOHN S. B. MONSELL   Arranged from J. MICHAEL HAYDN

The Rev. John S. B. Monsell's harvest hymn, "Sing to the Lord of harvest," was first published in the second edition of his *Hymns of Love and Praise,* 1866. He altered the first line to "Sing to the Lord of bounty," when he published it in his *Parish Hymnal,* 1873; but the original first line has survived.

TUNE: "Greenland" (See Nos. 1 and 6.)

282. Come, Ye Thankful People, Come

TUNE: "St. George's, Windsor"

HENRY ALFORD   GEORGE J. ELVEY

Dean Henry Alford's harvest hymn, "Come, ye thankful people, come," has proved to be the most popular of the many hymns he wrote. In his *Psalms and Hymns,* 1844, it had its first printing; but he revised it when he put it into his *Poetical Works,* 1865. Some revisions made by other hands he repudiated. (See No. 240.)

TUNE: "St. George's, Windsor" is the name of the church, where from 1835 to 1882 Sir George Job Elvey was organist, and one of the hymn-tunes he composed, while there, was named for this church. (See No. 80.)

283. The Beautiful, Bright Sunshine

TUNE: "Oliver"

ANONYMOUS   G. E. OLIVER

The authorship of this glad hymn of the summer-time, of home and of heaven, is unknown.

TUNE: The hymn-tune, "Oliver," takes its name from its composer, G. E. Oliver.

284. Summer Suns Are Glowing

TUNE: "Ruth"

WILLIAM WALSHAM HOW   SAMUEL SMITH

In *Church Hymns,* published by the Society for the Propagation of Christian Knowledge in 1871, Bishop William Walsham How's hymn, "Summer suns are glowing," was first printed. (See No. 88.)

TUNE: The tune, "Ruth," by the English organist, Samuel Smith, was composed and published in 1870. (See No. 262.)

285. We Have Heard the Joyful Sound

TUNE: "Jesus Saves"

PRISCILLA J. OWENS   WILLIAM J. KIRKPATRICK

Miss Priscilla J. Owens (1829-1899) was a teacher in the schools of Baltimore, Maryland, her birth-place. For a half century active in Sunday school work, she wrote many hymns for children. She composed her missionary hymn, "We have heard the joyful sound," for a missionary anniversary in her Sunday school, where it was sung to the tune of "Vive le Roi" from Meyerbeer's "The Huguenots." The tune to "Jesus Saves" was composed by William J. Kirkpatrick. (See No. 321.)

This is one of the hymns that is very effective when used antiphonally. Let the choir or a soloist sing the first phrase, the audience responding with "Jesus saves, Jesus saves." If the crowd is large, opposite sides or the audience and the gallery could sing antiphonally. It is a great hymn to sing in an evangelistic meeting.

286. Master, the Tempest Is Raging

MARY A. BAKER   Tune by H. R. PALMER

Mary A. Baker, author of "Master, the tempest is raging," has told the story of her hymn in these words:

Doctor Palmer requested me to prepare several songs on the subject of the current Sunday school lessons. One of the themes was "Christ Stilling the Tempest." It so expressed an experience I had recently passed through, that this hymn was the result. A very dear and only brother, a young man of rare loveliness and promise of character, had been laid in the grave, a victim of the same disease that had already taken father and mother. His death occurred under peculiarly distressing circumstances. He was more than a thousand miles away from home, seeking in the balmy air of the sunny south the healing that our colder climate could not give. Suddenly he grew worse. The writer was ill and could not go to him. For two weeks the long lines of telegraph wires carried back and forth messages between the dying brother and his waiting sisters, ere the final came which told us that our beloved brother was no longer a dweller on the earth. Although we mourned not as those without hope, and although I had believed in Christ in early childhood and had always desired to give the Master a consecrated and obedient life, I became wickedly rebellious at this dispensation of divine providence. But the Master's own voice stilled the tempest in my unsanctified heart, and brought it to the calm of a deeper faith and a more perfect trust.

This chorus offers splendid opportunity for good choral effects, by contrast. Change the markings that are usually found, singing the first phrase, "The winds and the waves shall obey Thy will," fortissimo. The following phrase render very softly, for contrast, "Peace be still, peace be still." Start the next phrase just as softly as possible, gradually increasing the volume to a double forte and the climax on "They all shall sweetly obey Thy will." Then, another sudden contrast by singing the "Peace be still" very softly; again double forte on "They all shall sweetly. obey Thy will," following with pianissimo singing of the last "Peace, peace be still." But, instead of letting the word, "still," die away, have the singers take a good breath before the last phrase, making a positive and tremendous swell on the last word, "still," breaking it abruptly at the height of the crescendo, then letting the singers hum softly the last two measures. This interpretation will produce a very lovely and unusual effect with only little explanation and rehearsal.

287. Come, We That Love the Lord

TUNE: *"We're Marching to Zion"*

ISAAC WATTS

ROBERT LOWRY

Dr. Isaac Watts entitled his hymn, "Come, we that love the Lord," in his *Hymns and Spiritual Songs,* 1707, "Heavenly Joy on Earth." He wrote the hymn's pronouns in the first person plural, as they are here given; though they are often sung in the second person plural,

> Come, ye that love the Lord,
> And let your joys be known.

TUNE: The tune was composed by the Rev. Dr. Robert Lowry, who was pastor of a number of prominent Baptist churches in America, and edited many successful Sunday school and evangelistic hymn-books. He is credited with having added the words of the chorus, "We're marching to Zion," to Doctor Watts's hymn.

This is one of the stirring martial songs of the church, good for any marching bodies of religious folks. One of my earliest impressions was of E. O. Excell, leading the folks of the old Lancaster camp-ground at Lancaster, Ohio, in their closing day's "March around Jerusalem," singing this song. It possibly had a very positive effect on my mind, even as a young boy, which eventually led me into this work of directing music.

288. Ring the Bells of Heaven

W. O. CUSHING   Tune by GEORGE F. ROOT

The tune, "The Little Octoroon," by the well-known composer, George F. Root, sent to William O. Cushing, led the latter to write his hymn, "Ring the bells of heaven." Cushing said of it:

> After receiving it, the melody ran in my head all day long, chiming and flowing in its sweet musical cadence. I wished greatly that I might secure the tune for work in the Sunday school and for other Christian purposes. When I heard the bells of heaven ringing over some sinner that had returned, it seemed like a glad day in heaven. Then the words, "Ring the bells of heaven," at once flowed down into the waiting melody. It was a beautiful and blessed experience, and the bells seem ringing yet.

George Frederick Root, Mus. Doc., who wrote this melody was a native of Sheffield, Massachusetts. He was born in 1820, and died in 1895. He was a most successful teacher of singing classes, and wrote many gospel hymn-tunes and also patriotic songs of the Civil War time, such as the "Battle Cry of Freedom" and "Just before the Battle, Mother."

This is another great song to sing at the close of the invitation, after folks have come forward. Using it as a special number for the children in the Sunday school, it is effective if the bells of the organ or the orchestra can be introduced.

289. "Man of Sorrows," What a Name!

P. P. BLISS   Tune by P. P. BLISS

The song, " 'Man of Sorrows,' what a name!" was written by P. P. Bliss, both in words and music, in 1876. Soon after writing it, he visited the State Prison at Jackson, Michigan, and made an address on "The Man of Sorrows," crowning his appeal with the singing of this song, which he had so recently composed. It had a wonderful effect upon his audience of prisoners, and many of them yielded their hearts to Jesus Christ. A few weeks later, Bliss was killed in a railroad wreck in Ashtabula, Ohio. (See No. 361.)

This can be made a most effective chorus number, and the interest and appreciation of a congregation can be tremendously increased by a careful interpretation of the real thought of the song. Read it over. Get the choir or the congregation really to appreciate its message. Start it with a stately rhythm, increase the tempo slightly with the second line, and then bring up the "Hallelujah" to a big fortissimo on the third syllable, cutting off rather abruptly after the fourth; and then after a slight pause, start very softly the last phrase, "What a Saviour," make a big swell on the "A" vowel in the word, "Saviour," bringing it up to the top of the wave, and then letting it diminish to a very soft tone as you finish the word. Because of the thought in the last verse, the tempo could be increased all the way through.

290. We Praise Thee, O God

TUNE: *"Revive Us Again"*

WILLIAM P. MACKAY   JOHN J. HUSBAND

The Rev. William Paton Mackay's hymn, "We praise Thee, O God," entitled "Revive Us Again," proved to be a popular song in the Moody and Sankey revival, as sung to the simple melody by John J. Husband. The tune is sometimes used to Doctor Bonar's "Rejoice and be glad" (1874).

Special interest can be created in this song by having different groups sing only the "Hallelujah." For instance, if your choir is being used in your song service, the choir could sing the chorus all the way through, the congregation joining only in the "Hallelujah" and the last phrase, "Revive us again."

291. What a Friend We Have in Jesus

JOSEPH SCRIVEN   Tune by CHARLES C. CONVERSE

The hymn, "What a Friend we have in Jesus," was written by a young man, Joseph Scriven, who at the time lived in Dublin, Ireland, where he was born in 1820. He was graduated from Trinity College, Dublin. Ira D. Sankey in his *Story of the Gospel Hymns* said that Scriven was engaged to marry a young lady, when just before the time set for the wedding she was accidentally drowned. This sad event led Scriven to discover what a Friend he had in Jesus, and his life he dedicated to His service. Later he moved to Canada, where he lived until his death, October 10, 1886, in Port Hope. The hymn was for a time mistakenly attributed in some hymnals to Dr. Horatius Bonar, who denied its authorship. Scriven sent the hymn to his mother and another copy to the mother of James Sackville in 1855, and gradually it found its way into print and eventually into wide popularity.

TUNE:. Charles C. Converse, composer of the tune to this hymn, was born in 1832 at Warren, Massachusetts; studied law, music and philosophy in Germany; and then practiced law in Boston. His musical interest is evidenced by many sacred and secular compositions which he wrote, none more popular than this simple little melody.

292. O Happy Day

PHILIP DODDRIDGE   Tune by EDWARD F. RIMBAULT

The Rev. Philip Doddridge gave to his hymn, beginning, "O happy day that fixed my choice," the title, "Rejoicing in our Covenant Engagements to God," and based its central thought on the text, 2 Chronicles 15, 15. It is likely that he had just finished preaching on this text when he wrote the hymn; as that was his frequent custom. It was not published until four years after his death in his *Hymns,* 1755, edited by J. Orton. This hymn has proved a great blessing in the evangelical churches. Prince Albert, consort of Queen Victoria, decreed that it should be sung whenever members of the royal family were confirmed. James Montgomery once said of it: "Blessed is the man who can take the words of this hymn and make them his own from similar experience." (See No. 94.)

TUNE: Edward F. Rimbault, Ph.D., LL.D., who was born in London, England, 1816, was the composer of the tune usually associated with "O Happy Day." He was not only an accomplished musician and composer, but became well known as a lecturer and writer on music. He was once offered the leadership of the department of music in Harvard University, but declined the honor. He died in 1876.

This is one of the very finest of all the songs to sing during the period of rejoicing after the invitation.

293. "Whosoever Heareth," Shout, Shout the Sound

P. P. BLISS   Tune by P. P. BLISS

Philip P. Bliss, the author and composer of " 'Whosoever heareth,' shout, shout the sound," heard with deep interest seven sermons of the text, John 3, 16, delivered by the English evangelist, Henry Morehouse, at Chicago, 1869-70. The preacher's description of the all-inclusiveness of God's invitation inspired Mr. Bliss to write this hymn at the conclusion of this series of sermons. (See No. 361.)

This is a great challenge song, and useful after almost any kind of a sermon.

294. I'm Pressing on the Upward Way

TUNE: *"Higher Ground"*

JOHNSON OATMAN, JR.   CHARLES H. GABRIEL

The Rev. Johnson Oatman, Jr., a Methodist Episcopal clergyman, was a member of the New Jersey Conference. He was a prolific writer of hymns. He died at Mount Holly, New Jersey, in 1926. The tune to "Higher Ground" was composed by Charles H. Gabriel. (See No. 330.)

When a sermon has been preached or an invitation given to members of the church to re-dedicate their lives for service, this is an exceptionally appropriate song to sing.

295. I Am Thine, O Lord

FANNY J. CROSBY   Tune by WILLIAM H. DOANE

Fanny J. Crosby, while visiting the home of Dr. William H. Doane in Cincinnati, Ohio, one late afternoon, just about sunset time, was talking with him on the nearness of God and His constant presence with us. This conversation and its influence upon her thoughts led her, that same evening before retiring, to write her hymn, "I am

Thine, O Lord," and its refrain, "Draw me nearer, nearer, blessed Lord." She showed it to Doctor Doane and he composed a tune which has carried the song on the voices of millions of worshippers. (See Nos. 307 and 314.)

This is one of the very best of all the songs of consecration.

296. Ho! My Comrades

TUNE: *"Hold the Fort"*

P. P. BLISS
                                                    P. P. BLISS

In May, 1870, Major D. W. Whittle in addressing a Sunday school gathering in Rockford, Illinois, gave a vivid description of General Sherman's advance in the Civil War to relieve the fort at Altoona Pass, which was being gallantly defended by General Corse and fifteen hundred Union troops against six thousand soldiers of General Hood's beleaguering Confederate army under General French. The fort being surrounded, the Confederates called upon Corse to surrender, and when he refused they advanced with a fierce attack and drove the Union troops into a small fort on top of the hill. Then one of them spied a signal, twenty miles away, on top of Kenesaw Mountain, which was interpreted thus: "Hold the fort, for I am coming. W. T. Sherman." They held the fort, although Corse and many of his troops were killed. The stirring story inspired Bliss to write the hymn, "Hold the Fort," which he sang for the first time the next day in Chicago Y. M. C. A., and taught the chorus to the audience. (See No. 361.)

Because of its appeal to the bravery of the human race, men love to sing this song. It is very effective as a challenge song, but in regular congregational singing it is good for men. Here is a thought for a bit of unusual use of this song: let some soloist or choir sing the first phrase of the chorus,

> "Hold the fort for I am coming,
> Jesus signals still."

Then let the congregation, waving their hands or their handkerchiefs, sing the response:

> "Wave the answer back to heaven,
> By Thy grace we will."

297. Yield Not to Temptation

H. R. PALMER   Tune by H. R. PALMER

Dr. H. R. Palmer, who wrote both the words and music of the song, "Yield not to temptation," has given this account of its composition:

This song was an inspiration. I was at work on the dry subject of 'Theory' when the complete idea flashed upon me, and I laid aside the theoretical work and hurriedly penned both words and music as fast as I could write them. I submitted them to the criticism of a friend afterward, and some changes were made in the third stanza, but the first two are exactly as they came to me.

This song should be used more often, and should be taught to young people. Never have they been faced with so many unusual and attractive temptations as today. The words of this song would be a tremendous help in strengthening their resolution at school, at work, or at play.

298. I Can Hear My Saviour Calling

TUNE: "*Where He Leads Me*"

E. W. BLANDLY   J. S. NORRIS

This is exceptionally good for the consecration meeting and is a very popular favorite with a great host of people. Do not sing this song hurriedly, its theme suggests a quiet, easy movement so as to get the full significance of this splendid poem.

299. Rescue the Perishing

FANNY J. CROSBY   Tune by WILLIAM H. DOANE

One summer's night of 1869 in New York city, Fanny Crosby visited one of the worst sections of the city to address the men who were gathered in a rescue mission. The thought came to her, while she was speaking, that "some mother's boy must be rescued that night or not at all." When she asked if there were a boy there who had wandered away from his mother's teaching, she made a plea that he speak to her at the close of the service. One young man did come forward and asked her: "Did you mean me? I promised my mother to meet her in heaven, but as I am now living that will be impossible." She prayed with him and he was joyfully converted. Dr. William H. Doane had recently asked her to write a hymn on the theme, "Rescue the Perishing"; and that night she wrote the hymn of that title, filled, as she was, with the thrill of the young man's conversion. (See No. 314.)

TUNE: Doctor Doane, when he received her hymn, composed its tune which has resounded through so many mission services the past six decades. (See No. 307.)

300. Sweet Hour of Prayer

W. W. Walford   Tune by William B. Bradbury

A blind minister in England, the Rev. William W. Walford, wrote in 1842 the most popular prayer hymn of the nineteenth century, "Sweet hour of prayer." He dictated it to the Rev. Thomas Salmon, who was then serving the Coleshill Congregational Church in Warwickshire, England, as pastor; and Salmon had it published in the New York *Observer* on September 13, 1845. Concerning Walford, Salmon has written:

During my residence in Colehill, Warwickshire, England, I became acquainted with W. W. Walford, the blind preacher, a man of obscure birth and connections and no education, but of strong mind and most retentive memory. In the pulpit he never failed to select a lesson well adapted to his subject, giving chapter and verse with unerring precision, and scarcely ever misplacing a word in his repetition of the Psalms, every part of the New Testament, the prophecies, and some of the histories, so as to have the reputation of knowing the whole Bible by heart.

TUNE: William B. Bradbury in 1859, finding this hymn of Walford's, wrote the tune that is so well adapted to the words, and they were together published in *Cottage Melodies,* 1859. (See No. 325.)

301. I Have a Saviour

S. O'Maley Cluff   Tune by Ira D. Sankey

S. O'Maley Cluff's hymn, "I have a Saviour, He's pleading in glory," was the second hymn which Ira D. Sankey, evangelistic singer, set to music. When Mr. Sankey was on his first visit to Ireland in 1874, with Dwight L. Moody, they found these words in a printed leaflet. Nothing was known about the author, but the sentiment of the song appealed so strongly to Mr. Sankey that he set about composing a tune for it, and had it completed in time to use it effectively and frequently in their meetings in London that same year.

This is another song that can be used antiphonally with splendid effect, letting the choir sing the first phrase of the chorus, the audience responding with the second. Or, if there is a crowd, let first one side sing and then the other, then the congregation, and then the folks in the gallery or the back part of the church, each singing a phrase of the chorus.

302. It May Not Be on the Mountain Height

TUNE: *"I'll Go Where You Want Me to Go"*

MARY BROWN   CARRIE E. ROUNSEFELL

One of the very first gospel songs that I ever heard after I left my home in the mountains of East Tennessee was Mary Brown's "I'll go where you want me to go." It was the singing of this song by a singer, named Ellis, in a young people's meeting at Ohio Wesleyan University, Delaware, Ohio, in 1897, that gave me my first urge to become a gospel singer.

Mrs. Carrie E. Rounsefell, who wrote the music, is a tiny woman who lives in Boston, Massachusetts. She used to do evangelistic work, and accompanied her singing with an old-fashioned zither. One day a friend handed her the words of this hymn and immediately a tune came to her and she struck a chord on her zither, and sang the song. Later, a friend of hers wrote it down for her and she had it published in a somewhat modified form. It has become a favorite at consecration meetings.

On the golf course in Florida, one day, Mr. John D. Rockefeller told me this was one of his favorite songs. He asked me to sing it for a group of folks who had gathered to meet and greet him. He joined and sang the chorus with us.

303. What Purpose Burns

ANONYMOUS   Tune by CHARLES H. GABRIEL

Dr. Norman E. Richardson at the School of Religious Education at Winona Lake, Indiana, was discussing hymns one day, when he made the statement that there were not any good hymns being written in this age. I was present and challenged the statement, and said: "You have not investigated: it can be done." To illustrate this I had a poem selected, "What purpose burns," and took it up to Charles H. Gabriel at the hotel that evening, saying: "I want a fine hymn-tune written for these words." The next morning it was finished, and I took it over to the chapel, and had a quartette sing it. They liked it. (See No. 330.)

304. Saviour, Draw Me to Thy Side

TUNE: *"Closer Still"*

DAVID J. BEATTIE   CHARLES H. GABRIEL

David J. Beattie, author of "Saviour, draw me to Thy side," lives in London, England. When I first went over the manuscript of "Closer Still" with Charles H. Gabriel, the latter was so much stirred that there were tears in his eyes, and when he came to compose a tune he endeavored to express in the musical setting this deep emotion which the hymn first stirred in him. (See No. 330.)

305. Shall We Gather at the River

ROBERT LOWRY   Tune by ROBERT LOWRY

The Rev. Robert Lowry, who wrote both words and music of "Shall we gather at the river," on a July afternoon in 1864, in his home on Ellicott Place, Brooklyn, New York, has made this comment on the song:

It is brass-band music, has a march movement, and for that reason has become popular, though, for myself, I do not think much of it. Yet on several occasions I have been deeply moved by the singing of this very hymn. Coming from Harrisburg to Lewisburg once I got into a car filled with half-drunken lumbermen. Suddenly one of them struck up, "Shall we gather at the river?" and they sang it over and over again, repeating the chorus in a wild, boisterous way. I did not think so much of the music then, as I listened to those singers; but I did think that perhaps the spirit of the hymn, the words so flippantly uttered, might somehow survive and be carried forward into the lives of those careless men, and ultimately lift them upward to the realization of the hope expressed in the hymn.

(See No. 287.)

306. I Will Sing of My Redeemer

TUNE: *"My Redeemer"*

P. P. BLISS

JAMES McGRANAHAN

P. P. Bliss, after writing his song, "I will sing of my Redeemer," sent it to his friend and colleague in the work of evangelistic singing, James McGranahan, with the request that he write a tune for it. When Mr. Bliss suddenly met his death in a railroad wreck, 1876, his place was taken by Mr. McGranahan as the singer in the evangelistic meetings of Major D. W. Whittle. (See No. 361.)

307. Take the Name of Jesus with You

LYDIA BAXTER

Tune by WILLIAM H. DOANE

Miss Lydia Baxter, born in Petersburg, New York, September 2, 1809, was converted while a girl and joined the Baptist Church. Later she moved to New York city. For years she was an invalid, confined to her room; but in her chamber of suffering she wrote her song, "Take the name of Jesus with you," which was written in 1870, and the following year was published in a hymnal, prepared by Dr. William H. Doane, who wrote the tune for these words.

Dr. William Howard Doane, born in Preston, Connecticut, February 3, 1832, early joined the Baptist Church, became a choir leader, and engaged in the manufacture of machinery through which he became quite wealthy. His music books, cantatas, and gospel hymntunes (forty books and twenty-three hundred compositions) justified Denison University in awarding him a musical doctorate. He died in 1909.

308. When You My Jesus Understand

TUNE: *"When You Know Jesus, Too"*

INA DULEY OGDON   B. D. ACKLEY

Mrs. Ina Duley Ogdon, author of "When you my Jesus understand," lives in Lambertville, Michigan. About the time when Mrs. Ogdon was preparing herself for work among the Chautauqua circuits, one day her father was brought home, seriously injured as the result of an automobile accident, which made him an invalid. This compelled her to give up her cherished ambition to enter the Chautauqua platform. At first, she could not be reconciled to this sacrifice of her plans. But as the added duties of the home claimed her more and more, the spirit of rebellion grew less, and gradually she began to be reconciled. It was during this period that she wrote, "Brighten the corner where you are." Her trouble and disappointment, however, still worried her, and in the effort to find release she wrote her song, "Though your heart may be heavy with sorrow and care" ("Carry your cross with a smile"). When finally she conquered her own wilfulness completely, and became fully reconciled to the will of God, she wrote as an expression of her newly-found peace the song, "When you my Jesus understand."

Several years ago the writer of the words of this song had worked the entire day to write a song for which the publisher had given the title and the music. For some time, at every opportunity, attention had been given this piece of work; but on this particular day, she had concentrated on the task, hoping to have the composition ready for the publisher,—a painstaking, as well as a fascinating and loving experience.

Just after completing it, and offering a prayer for God's blessing to go with it, she was called to have dinner with her family. As she laid aside her work, she was very weary, but very happy, in work done for the Saviour. She was thinking of the joy of His service, when, as often, the wonder came to her that any should hesitate to trust and serve Him. Then the thought came, "All will come to Him and love Him when they understand," with the suggestion of the helpfulness of a song of that logic and the irresistible desire to try to write such an appeal at once.

She asked her family to excuse her from dinner; she again sat down at her desk and, working into the morning hours, she wrote the song as it is now used by so many consecrated, soul-winning singers,—a humble, little song; but with great power, bearing, as it does, the simple testimony of joy, peace and love, and the fulfillment of all promise, "When you know Jesus, too."

TUNE: Mrs. Ogdon sent the words to B. D. Ackley, who set it to music. Of this union of words and melody the composer has said: "There was always an appeal in these words to my heart, and it was not difficult to set them to music." This was adopted as the favorite song by the men of the Billy Sunday Business Men's Club of Syracuse, New York.

309. I Must Tell Jesus

E. A. HOFFMAN   Tune by E. A. HOFFMAN

The Rev. Elisha A. Hoffman, a Congregational minister, was serving a pastorate in Lebanon, Pennsylvania. He was called upon to visit a parishoner who was in great trouble. He tried to comfort her by telling her of the great love of Christ. He urged that she could find no help until she reached a complete repentance through Jesus. Suddenly she screamed: "I must tell Jesus!" This led to her conversion, and impelled him to write on the theme of her words the hymn, "I must tell Jesus all of my trials."

310. I Need Jesus

GEORGE O. WEBSTER   CHARLES H. GABRIEL

The Rev. George O. Webster is pastor of a community church in New York state. In 1923, sitting on the porch, one afternoon, just as the sun was sinking in the west, he fell to thinking about the current religious controversy between the Fundamentalists and the Modernists; and he remarked to himself: "How much they all need Jesus!" And suddenly there came the thought, "How much *I* need Jesus!" Then in the swift setting of the sun he composed the lines of his hymn, "I need Jesus." Charles H. Gabriel set it to music. (See No. 330.)

People get a new appreciation of this song when you remind them that it tells of the world's greatest need, the need of the individual, the need of organizations, the need of nations and the world. And every problem between men, governments and nations would be solved by the principles and plan for living that Jesus gave to us.

311. My Jesus, I Love Thee

London Hymn Book   Tune by A. J. GORDON

The Rev. Dr. A. J. Gordon, a prominent Baptist clergyman in Boston, Massachusetts, found the anonymous lines, "My Jesus, I love Thee," in a London Hymn Book and set to them the melody which has made the song popular in America.

This can be used very effectively as a duet between the tenor and soprano, and a very pleasing effect can be secured from your congregation sometimes by letting the women sing the melody and all the men sing the tenor.

312. When Peace, Like a River

H. G. SPAFFORD   Tune by P. P. BLISS

In 1873 the steamship, "Ville de Havre," bound for France, struck a large sailing vessel in mid-ocean and in a half hour sank with nearly all on board. Few were saved, among them Mrs. Horatio G. Spafford, wife of a Chicago business man. When she learned that the ship would surely sink, she brought her four children out of the berths to the deck, where they all knelt in prayer. All of the children were lost. One of the sailors, named Lockburn, after the ship sank, found Mrs. Spafford floating in the water, and rescued her. When she landed in Wales, she cabled to her husband the grim message, "Saved alone." He understood its import, that their children were lost. On Spafford's arrival in England to bring his wife home, Dwight L. Moody left his Edinburgh meetings to comfort them, and had the satisfaction of hearing Spafford say, "It is well; the will of God be done." Out of that experience Spafford wrote the hymn, "When peace, like a river, attendeth my way," with its refrain, "It is well, it is well with my soul." The music was written by P. P. Bliss. (See No. 361.)

313. Jesus, Rose of Sharon

IDA A. GUIREY   Tune by CHARLES H. GABRIEL

The song, "Jesus, Rose of Sharon," written by Miss Ida A. Guirey was set to music by Charles H. Gabriel. (See No. 330.)

Here is one of the loveliest hymns it has been our privilege to introduce. Read over the poem and get the full import of this wonderful message—your choir will find this a very fine number to use.

314. Tell Me the Story of Jesus

FANNY J. CROSBY   Tune by JOHN R. SWENEY

Frances Jane Crosby was the name given at her birth, March 24, 1820, to the blind hymn-writer, whom we have known as Fanny Crosby. After becoming a graduate from, and a teacher in, the New York Institution for the Blind for some years (1847-1858), she married a blind man, Alexander Van Alstyne, who lived until 1902. Her poems early attracted attention and she read some of them before Congress in Washington. In 1864 she began to write for William B. Bradbury a series of Sunday school hymns. These and evangelistic songs she continued to produce throughout her life, until she had written over eight thousand hymns. During most of her life her home was in New York city, where she was a member of Old John Street Methodist Episcopal Church, but her latter days were spent in Bridgeport, Connecticut, where she died in 1915 in her ninety-fifth year. She was always fond of children, and one of her successful songs for them was, "Tell me the story of Jesus," set to music by her friend, John R. Sweney. (See No. 320.)

During the World War, I sang the song, "Tell me the story of Jesus," to many groups of soldiers in France,—in the old, shell-torn barracks, in dugouts where there was only a little candle with which to see the words, or in the open as the line of soldiers, marching to the front, would stop for rest; and once, on October 4, 1918, in the Argonne Forest, just as a big drive had started. But no matter where I sang this song, the soldier boys would take off their dirty service caps or hang their trench helmets on their arms and remain perfectly quiet. There was no other song that I sang with this same effect. Many men have met me since the war and referred to the unusual situations in which it was sung and the impression the song made upon them at the time.

315. Lovely to the Outward Eye

W. RUSSELL BOWIE   Tune by J. B. HERBERT

The Rev. Dr. W. Russell Bowie, who is rector of Grace Protestant Episcopal Church, New York city, is the author of "Lovely to the outward eye." (See No. 147.)

TUNE: Dr. J. B. Herbert, who wrote the tune to this hymn, was a prominent United Presbyterian layman in Monmouth, Illinois, where he was serving at the time of his death. He was an outstanding musical leader in his denomination. He was the composer also of "The Brewer's Big Horses" and "Molly and I and the Baby." He was one of the most prominent teachers of singing schools throughout the west and the south. His books on theoretical subjects have been used in nearly every country. He directed the music in many United Presbyterian churches and conventions, and set many of the psalms to music. He wrote many successful gospel songs in addition to his setting of the psalms. During the last years of his life, he was making special efforts to find and arrange more singable tunes to some of the wonderful hymns that have not been used much because the tunes originally given to them were not so singable. Doctor Herbert was a man of unusual character and lovely spirit.

316. Saviour, Thy Dying Love

S. D. PHELPS   Tune by ROBERT LOWRY

About 1875, the Rev. Sylvanus D. Phelps, a Baptist clergyman (born in Sheffield, Connecticut, May 15, 1816), and a graduate from Brown University (1844), published in a Boston religious periodical, *The Watchman and Reflector,* his hymn, "Saviour, Thy dying love."

TUNE: When the Rev. Dr. Robert Lowry (see No. 287) was preparing his hymn-book, *Pure Gold,* along with Dr. William H. Doane, he asked Mr. Phelps to furnish some hymns for the book. Among them was this hymn, for which Dr. Lowry composed the tune and he published them in his hymnal. Years later, when Mr. Phelps reached his seventieth birthday (nine years before his death in 1895), Dr. Lowry wrote to him:

It is worth living seventy years, even if nothing comes of it but one such hymn as "Saviour, Thy dying love." Happy is the man who can produce one song which the world will keep on singing after its author shall have passed away.

317. I Need Thee Every Hour

ANNIE S. HAWKS   Tune by ROBERT LOWRY

Mrs. Annie Sherwood Hawks, born in Hoosack, New York, May, 1835, was married in 1859 to Charles Hial, who died in 1888. She wrote verses when she was only fourteen years old. In 1872 her most famous hymn, "I need Thee every hour," was written in Brooklyn. She was encouraged in her hymn-writing by her pastor, the Rev. Dr. Robert Lowry. She has given the following account of its composition:

Whenever my attention is called to it, I am conscious of great satisfaction in the thought that I was permitted to write the hymn, "I need Thee every hour," and that it was wafted out to the world on the wings of love and joy, rather than under the stress of a great personal sorrow, with which it has so often been associated in the minds of those who sing it.

I remember well the morning, many years ago, when in the midst of the daily cares of my home, then in a distant city, I was so filled with the sense of nearness to the Master that, wondering how one could live without Him either in joy or pain, these words, "I need Thee every hour," were ushered into my mind, the thought at once taking full possession of me. Seating myself by the open window in the balmy air of the bright June day, I caught my pencil, and the words were soon committed to paper, almost as they are being sung today.

TUNE: Mrs. Hawks's pastor, Dr. Robert Lowry, composed the tune for these words and included it in a small collection of songs, which he and Dr. W. H. Doane prepared for the National Baptist Sunday School Association meeting in Cincinnati, Ohio, in November, 1872. (See No. 287.)

318. Pass Me Not, O Gentle Saviour

FANNY J. CROSBY   Tune by WILLIAM H. DOANE

Mrs. Fanny J. Crosby Van Alstyne, the blind poet, in 1868, was asked by Dr. William H. Doane to write a hymn on the theme, "Pass me not, O gentle Saviour." Taking the theme as first line, she wrote this hymn and gave it to Doctor Doane, who composed the melody for it. Ira D. Sankey, who popularized it by singing the hymn in the meetings conducted by Dwight L. Moody, used to tell the story of one man who was converted through the singing of this song:

(My conversion) was all through that hymn we have just sung. I was working on the canal at G——, and there was a meeting being held at the Mariners' Chapel, near by. The words floated out over the water, and from the tug where I was working I could hear them plainly enough. When they were just going to sing these lines,

> While on others Thou art calling,
>   Do not pass me by,

a great fear came over me, and I thought, "Oh, if the Lord were to pass me by, how terrible it would be." Then and there, on the tug, I cried out: "O Lord, do not pass me by." And he didn't pass me by. I am saved.

As you compare the melody of this song with the lovely and popular song of Hawaii, "Aloha Oe," you will find a great similarity; and it is altogether possible that the melody of the Hawaiian song was suggested by the singing of this song, when the missionaries went to Hawaii. (See Nos. 307 and 314.)

319. The Name of Jesus

W. C. MARTIN   Tune by E. S. LORENZ

To the hymn, "The Name of Jesus," by Evangelist Martin, the Rev. Dr. Edmund S. Lorenz composed one of the best-known of hundreds of gospel hymn-tunes that have come from his pen. Born in Stark County, Ohio, July 13, 1854, Doctor Lorenz was graduated from Otterbein University; afterwards doing graduate work in Union Biblical Seminary, Yale Theological School (B.D.) and the University of Leipzig. After serving as pastor in the United Brethren Church, he became president of Lebanon Valley College. An illness of three years terminated his college work, and from a small beginning in music publishing gradually he developed the Lorenz Publishing Company of which he is president. He founded and published the *Choir Leader* and *Choir Herald,* musical periodicals, and has published many song books, including a large number of hymns and tunes of his own writing.

320. More About Jesus

E. E. HEWITT   Tune by JOHN R. SWENEY

Miss Eliza Edmunds Hewitt, born in Philadelphia, June 28, 1851, after graduation from high school, became a teacher. A spinal malady, however, made her an invalid for many years. Later an improvement in her condition made it possible for her to take a course in English literature. Her poems for children attracted the attention of John R. Sweney, who set some of them to music and published them. It was this relation that led him to discover one of her best hymns, "More about Jesus I would know," and he set it to music.

Born in West Chester, Pennsylvania, December 31, 1837, Sweney studied music under Professor Bauer, mastering violin and piano, and becoming a choir leader. In the Civil War he conducted the Delaware Third Regiment band; and after the war for a quarter of a century taught music in the Pennsylvania Military Academy, at Chester (from which he received the degrees of Mus. Bac. and Mus. Doc.). He became well known as song leader at summer religious assemblies, notably Ocean Grove, New Jersey, and his gospel hymn-tunes and hymnals (in which he collaborated largely with William J. Kirkpatrick) had a wide circulation. He died April 10, 1899.

321. 'Tis So Sweet to Trust in Jesus

LOUISA M. R. STEAD   Tune by WILLIAM J. KIRKPATRICK

William J. Kirkpatrick (1838-1917), a native of Duncannon, Pennsylvania, a regimental musician in the Civil

War, an organist, gospel singer, and composer, editor and publisher of gospel songs, wrote the tune to the hymn, " 'Tis so sweet to trust in Jesus," in his home in Philadelphia. The words of this hymn were the keynote of his life to the very end. On the last day of his life, in a call on George W. Sanville in the Philadelphia office of The Rodeheaver Company, he was trying to decide whether to sell some of his copyrighted songs. After much thought he went to his home saying that he would return the next day and make a decision. That night, in the library of his home, he was working quite late upon the manuscript of a new hymn. His wife twice awakened from her sleep and went to his door, and found that he seemed to be all right, although wrestling late with the writing of a hymn. The third time she came to his room, she found that he had passed away. But on the floor, near his lifeless body, there rested the manuscript of the hymn he had been writing. It was eloquent of the spirit in which he had passed to the life beyond. Here is the poem that he had been working on before the call came to come home:

> Just as Thou wilt, Lord, this is my cry,
> Just as Thou wilt to live or to die;
> I am Thy Servant, Thou knowest best,
> Just as Thou wilt, Lord, labor or rest.

On the reverse side was a second stanza as follows:

> Just as Thou wilt, Lord, which shall it be,
> Life everlasting working for me;
> Or shall I tarry here at Thy feet?
> Just as Thou wilt, Lord, whatever is meet.

And with this his last message, Mr. Kirkpatrick went home to be with God.

322. I Gave My Life for Thee

FRANCES R. HAVERGAL   Tune by P. P. BLISS

Miss M. V. G. Havergal, sister of the hymnist, has given this account of the writing of Miss Frances Ridley Havergal's hymn, "I gave My life for thee":

In F. R. H.'s mss. copy, she gives this title, "I did this for thee; what hast thou done for Me?" Motto placed under the picture of our Saviour in the study of a German divine. On January 10, 1858, she had come in weary, and sitting down she read the motto, and the lines of her hymn flashed upon her. She wrote them in pencil on a scrap of paper. Reading them over she thought them so poor that she tossed them into the fire, but they fell out untouched. Showing them some months after to her father, he encouraged her to preserve them, and wrote the tune *Baca* specially for them. The hymn was printed on a leaflet, 1859, and in *Good Words*, February, 1860. Published also in *The Ministry of Song*, 1869.

The author of the hymn made this comment also on the hymn in her *Memoirs*:

I was so overwhelmed on Sunday at hearing three of my hymns touchingly sung in Perry Church, I never before realized the high privilege of writing for the "great congregation," especially when they sang "I gave My life for thee," to my father's tune, *Baca*.

The first line of the hymn is sometimes rendered, "Thy life was given for me," and the pronouns throughout are altered accordingly. (See No. 110.)

P. P. Bliss wrote this melody for the words. (See No. 361.)

323. Saviour, More than Life to Me

FANNY J. CROSBY   Tune by WILLIAM H. DOANE

The hymn, "Saviour, more than life to me," by Fanny J. Crosby, appeared first in her book, *Brightest and Best*, 1875, having the title, "Jesus, All in All." Ira D. Sankey told the story of its writing in these words:

The tune preceded the words in this instance. It was in 1875 that Mr. Doane sent the tune to Fanny Crosby and requested her to write a hymn entitled: "Every Day and Hour." Her response in the form of this hymn gave the blind hymn-writer great comfort and filled her heart with joy. She felt sure that God would bless the hymn to many hearts. Her hope has been most fully verified, for millions have been refreshed and strengthened as they have sung it. At the suggestion of Mr. D. W. McWilliams, who was superintendent of Dr. Cuyler's Sunday School for twenty-five years, it was put into *Gospel Hymns*.

(See Nos. 307 and 314.)

324.   On a Hill Far Away

TUNE: *"The Old Rugged Cross"*

GEORGE BENNARD   GEORGE BENNARD

The hymn, "The Old Rugged Cross," was written by the Rev. George Bennard, a Michigan evangelist in the Methodist Episcopal church.   During a revival meeting in upper Michigan, while a great spiritual tide was running, the author was in deep thought, reading about the crucifixion of Jesus Christ, when he was stirred to write these lines.

When Miss Alice Shaefer went to China as a missionary she took with her some phonograph records.   One day at the Ming Sam School for the blind in Canton, she was playing some of these records for the other teachers there, and among them the record of "The Old Rugged Cross." A little blind girl there was in the midst of one of the curious fits of temper, to which she was subject; when, hearing the song, she stopped and quietly crept to the side of one of the teachers.   Puzzled, the teacher brought her to the phonograph, the next time she had a fit of temper, and put on the same record.   Immediately the child became quiet.   She could not understand the words, but there was something in the rhythm or melody or harmony of that song which quieted the girl's disordered nervous system.   What an illustration it is of how the disordered, distraut nervous system of the whole world could be put into order by the teachings that circle around "The Old Rugged Cross."   One young lady asked that we sing it on a radio program for her father.   Later she told me of the death of her father and how much the song had meant to him.   When the doctors told him that he had a cancer and could not get well, he began calling his cancer his "Old Rugged Cross," and it was on the supporting arms of this "Old Rugged Cross" that he was carried into the presence of his God.   Broadcasting stations received more requests for the singing of this, than for any other song that is sung on the air, popular or otherwise.

325. Saviour, Like a Shepherd, Lead Us

DOROTHY ANN THRUPP   Tune by WILLIAM B. BRADBURY

The evidence for the writing of this hymn points to Dorothy Ann Thrupp as author, though this is not at all certain. Miss Thrupp, if indeed she be the author, was fond of writing hymns for children. Born in London, England, June 20, 1779, she was the daughter of Joseph Thrupp of Paddington Green. She published many volumes of hymns and poems, among them being *Hymns for the Young,* 1830, in the fourth edition of which, 1836, this hymn and all the other hymns attributed to her appeared. She died in London, December 14, 1847.

William B. Bradbury, who composed the winsome tune for these words, was a native of York, Maine (October 6, 1816), studied music in Boston, where he became a choir singer and organist, later serving in Brooklyn and New York city churches. With Doctor Hastings he published *The Young Choir,* 1841. In 1847 he studied music in Leipzig, Germany; and, returning to this country, began a remarkable career as music editor and publisher (fifty-nine books), composer, manufacturer of pianos, choral conductor and teacher. He died in Montclair, New Jersey, January 8, 1868.

326. There Is a Green Hill Far Away

CECIL F. ALEXANDER   Tune by J. B. HERBERT

Mrs. Cecil Frances Alexander, wife of Bishop Alexander of Derry and Raphoe, Ireland, wrote a series of hymns for children, based on phrases of the Apostles' Creed, and published them in *Hymns for Little Children,* 1848. One of these, to illustrate the words, "Suffered under Pontius Pilate, was crucified, dead, and buried," was composed in 1847, while Mrs. Alexander was visiting the bedside of a little girl, a member of her class, who was seriously ill. She is pre-eminently known as a successful writer of hymns for children. (See No. 59.)

J. B. Herbert made the musical setting of the hymn. (See No. 315.)

327. There Is a Name I Love to Hear (Jesus)

INA DULEY OGDON   Tune by B. D. ACKLEY

Mrs. Ina Duley Ogdon wrote the song, "There is a Name I love to hear." Her own account of its composition is this:

The inspiration for this song was the outgrowth of the morning hour of worship. Thoughts of the sweet music of His name, falling like balm of healing into hearts of sorrow and care, of the soul-inspiring picture of an all-loving, all-forgiving Saviour, guiding us through the perplexities of the long, often hard, days of His own burden, borne from the cradle at Bethlehem to the cross on Calvary, and of the joy of an abiding place in Him, grew at last into the blessed privilege of sending out the heart message to others. (See No. 308.)

TUNE: The melody to these words was written by B. D. Ackley just prior to a visit to the evangelistic meetings in Springfield, Ohio, 1911. He took it to Springfield and played it over for me in the parlor of the home where we were staying. "Billy" Sunday was present, and was so impressed by it that he became enthusiastic over it, and begged the composer to let him have it for use in his meetings; where, indeed, it has been frequently used through the years. (See No. 369.)

328. Ye Who Wander

E. E. REXFORD   Tune by B. D. ACKLEY

The Rev. "Billy" Sunday in one of his sermons in 1909 used the phrase, "How you will love Him when you know Him!" B. D. Ackley, hearing this, was impressed deeply by the idea, thus uttered, and felt that it could be made the theme of a song. Accordingly, he made a rough outline of the chorus during evangelistic meetings in Springfield, Illinois, and sent it to Dr. Eben E. Rexford, asking him to write the words of a hymn, centering about this phrase.

The Springfield meetings closed in May, and Mr. Ackley with Dr. Glenn Frank (now president of the University of Wisconsin) and others went on to Union, Iowa, for a four-weeks' session of meetings. By this time Doctor

Rexford had sent the completed hymn to Mr. Ackley, who describes the composing of the tune as follows:

It was during the Union, Iowa, meetings that one day I went into the basement of a little church, where it was cool—for it was warm weather at the time—and I spent hours working out the tune to the verse, which never did quite satisfy me. But that is true of most of our work. We try our best, and yet there is always something within us that is never entirely satisfied with what we are able to do—a song in our soul that we never can set down in notes.

Mr. Rexford was the author of the famous popular song, "Silver threads among the gold." (See No. 369.)

329. Joys Are Flowing Like a River

TUNE: *"Holy Quietness"*

M. P. FERGUSON   Arranged from W. S. MARSHALL

The hymn by M. P. Ferguson, "Joys are flowing," has been set to a tune, "Holy Quietness," arranged from W. S. Marshall.

This is one of the loveliest and most useful of all Quiet Hour and Devotional Period songs.

330. Lord, as of Old at Pentecost

TUNE: *"Pentecostal Power"*

CHARLOTTE G. HOMER   CHARLES H. GABRIEL

Both words and music of "Lord, as of old at Pentecost," were written by Charles H. Gabriel (for "Charlotte G. Homer" is now recognized as one of his favorite pseudonyms). Gabriel was born August 18, 1859, in Iowa. At seventeen years he held singing classes in many different states of the Union, later settling in California. In a sense, he has been the foremost gospel hymn-tune writer of his generation, composing not only hundreds of tunes, but a great many that have gone into large circulation. It is said that his "Glory Song" has been printed over 20,000,000 times. He wrote fourteen books of anthems, and composed many cantatas and sacred operettas, besides editing over one hundred festival programs. After living for many years in Chicago, he has retired again to California.

331. Marvelous Grace of Our Loving Lord

JULIA H. JOHNSTON   Tune by D. B. TOWNER

Miss Julia H. Johnston, who in 1910 wrote "Marvelous grace of our loving Lord," lives in Peoria, Illinois. She is a prolific writer, especially in the field of Primary Sunday school lessons, golden text talks with mothers, editorials, articles and poems. She has published a number of volumes. Her hymn-writing, however, she regards as a most sacred task, and already over five hundred of them have been printed. She has for years been in charge of the Beginners' Department in the Sunday school in her home city.

TUNE: Dr. D. Brink Towner, composer of the tune to "Marvelous grace," was born in Rome, Pennsylvania, March 5, 1850. In 1870 he was in charge of the music of the Centenary Methodist Episcopal Church, Binghamton, New York; in 1882, in the York Street Methodist Church, Cincinnati, Ohio; in 1885 joined D. L. Moody as a singer in his evangelistic work; in 1893 became superintendent of music in the Moody Bible Institute, Chicago. A great singer, he was also composer of many gospel songs.

332. When All My Labors

TUNE: *"Glory Song"*

CHARLES H. GABRIEL   CHARLES H. GABRIEL

"The Glory Song" was written in 1900 by the famous gospel song writer, Charles H. Gabriel; and he also composed its joyous tune. He once wrote of it:

The most remarkable fact concerning the song is that it stands today (1912), note for note, word for word, as I sent it to the printer twelve years ago. It has been translated into more than twenty different languages and dialects, and over twenty millions of copies have been printed.

The song was given wings all over the world, as it was sung by the late Charles M. Alexander in his evangelistic campaigns with Evangelist R. A. Torrey. (See No. 330.)

333. Far Away in the Depths of My Spirit

W. D. CORNELL. Altered   Tune by W. G. COOPER

The hymn, "Far away in the depths of my spirit," by W. D. Cornell has been altered from its original form. Set to music by W. G. Cooper, it has proven to be an effective and popular song on the peace of the soul.

334. True-Hearted, Whole-Hearted

FRANCES R. HAVERGAL   Tune by GEORGE C. STEBBINS

Miss Frances Ridley Havergal's hymn, "True-hearted, whole-hearted, faithful and loyal," she first published in her fourth volume, *Loyal Responses,* in 1878, and it later appeared in the *Universal Hymn Book,* 1885. (See No. 110.)

TUNE: The song owes much of its success to the finely rhythmical melody composed for it by George Coles Stebbins. He was born in Orleans County, New York, February 26, 1846. In 1870 he became musical director of the First Baptist Church, Chicago, and four years later became associated with D. L. Moody and Ira D. Sankey. In 1876 he went to Boston, taking charge of the music in Dr. A. J. Gordon's Baptist Church, and later in the Tremont Temple. He later renewed his association with Moody and other evangelists in their campaigns. He wrote many successful gospel tunes, besides "True-hearted," such as "Saved by Grace," "In the secret of His presence," "Take time to be holy," and the hymn-tune, "Saviour, breathe an evening blessing."

335. All the Way My Saviour Leads Me

FANNY J. CROSBY   Tune by ROBERT LOWRY

One day Fanny Crosby (afterwards Mrs. Alexander Van Alstyne), the blind poet, was desperately in need of five dollars for some necessary purpose, and did not know how to get it. So she prayed to the Lord for it. Soon afterwards a gentleman called at her home, shook hands with her, and after greeting her immediately went out.

But after shaking his hand, she found a five dollar bill in her hand. She added in telling the story:

> I have no way to account for this, except to believe that God, in answer to my prayer, put it into the heart of this good man to bring me the money. My first thought, after finding out the pecuniary value of this little silken reminder of friendship and regard, was, "In what a wonderful way the Lord helps me!" I immediately wrote the hymn, and Dr. Robert Lowry, the famous clergyman-hymn-writer, set it to music.

(See Nos. 287 and 314.)

336.   Be Not Aweary, for Labor Will Cease

CHARLOTTE G. HOMER   Tune by CHARLES H. GABRIEL

When the composer and author of this song, Charles H. Gabriel (whose pseudonym was sometimes "Charlotte G. Homer"), handed the manuscript to me, it bore this legend in his handwriting, "This is a song that will be sung around the world." On only one other song of his has he ever written such a prophetic note, and that was on "The Glory Song." Its success has amply fulfilled his prophecy, for it has literally been sung "around the world," bearing the message of that "Bright Morning." (See No. 330.)

337.   Be Not Dismayed, Whate'er Betide

TUNE: *"God Will Take Care of You"*

MRS. C. D. MARTIN   W. S. MARTIN

Words and music of "God will take care of you" were written respectively by husband and wife, the Rev. and Mrs. W. S. Martin. Mrs. Martin was suddenly stricken with appendicitis. Gangrene, they afterwards found, had already set in. She was rushed to the hospital for an operation. Her husband stayed with her until time for the ether to be administered. Worrying more about her husband's predicament, caused by her sudden illness, she finally leaned over to him and said: "Never mind, Hubby; God will take care of you!" During her period of convalescence these words recurred to her and phrased themselves into the hymn lines:

> Be not dismayed, whate'er betide,
> God will take care of you.

Sitting at the melodeon in their home, the Rev. W. S. Martin composed the tune, to which it is now sung around the world.

338. Blessed Assurance, Jesus Is Mine

FANNY J. CROSBY   Tune by MRS. JOSEPH F. KNAPP

The writing of the hymn, "Blessed assurance, Jesus is mine," by Fanny J. Crosby was promoted by the composition of a tune by Mrs. Joseph F. Knapp of New York city, who brought it to Miss Crosby and played it over for her, two or three times. Then she asked: "Fanny, what does that tune say to you?" After thinking of it for a few moments, Miss Crosby replied: "Blessed assurance, Jesus is mine!" That phrase she soon developed into a hymn, set to Mrs. Knapp's tune, and they have been widely used together ever since then. (See No. 314.)

339. Blessed Lord, in Thee Is Refuge

HERBERT BOOTH   Tune by W. OWEN

Herbert Booth, the writer of the hymn, "Blessed Lord, in Thee is refuge," was the son of Commander William Booth, founder of the Salvation Army, himself an active leader in his father's remarkable organization. Set to a tune by W. Owen, a Welsh composer, it has been frequently sung, not only by the Salvation Army throughout the world, but also by many of the evangelical churches in this country and England.

340. Brightly Beams Our Father's Mercy

TUNE: "Lower Lights"

P. P. BLISS

P. P. BLISS

Dwight L. Moody, the evangelist, was addressing an audience in which P. P. Bliss was included, when he told the following story:

On a dark, stormy night, when the waves rolled like mountains and not a star was to be seen, a boat, rocking and plunging, neared the Cleveland harbor. "Are you sure this is Cleveland?" asked the captain, seeing only one light from the lighthouse. "Quite sure, sir," replied the pilot. "Where are the lower lights?" "Gone out, sir." "Can you make the harbor?" "We must or perish, sir!" With a strong hand and a brave heart the old pilot turned the wheel. But alas, in the darkness he missed the channel, and with a crash upon the rocks the boat was shivered, and many a life lost in a watery grave. Brethren, the Master will take care of the great lighthouse; let us keep the lower lights burning!

This incident, which thrilled Mr. Bliss as he heard it, prompted him to write the words and music of his famous song, "Let the lower lights be burning." (See No. 361.)

The chorus of this song can be used with splendid effect antiphonally. Let the whole congregation sing the first phrase of the chorus, then the last five or six rows of the people in the gallery sing the second phrase, the whole crowd again singing the third phrase, and the smaller group again responding with the last one.

341. Dear Lord, Take Up the Tangled Strands

MRS. F. G. BURROUGHS   Tune by B. D. ACKLEY

The beautiful prayer hymn, "Dear Lord, take up the tangled strands," by Mrs. F. G. Burroughs was for some time in the possession of Professor William J. Kirkpatrick in manuscript form before it was published. He gave it to Mr. B. D. Ackley, who was helping us in the "Billy" Sunday campaign in Paterson, New Jersey, in 1915. Mr. Ackley was stirred by its beauty and has since said of it: "The words of this poem are wonderfully strong." He set it to music and before the close of the Paterson campaign turned over words and music to me for use in the meetings. (See No. 369.)

This poem is exceptional and worthy of more than ordinary study. The choir will also find the tune especially beautiful and effective if they will work it up carefully and use it as a prayer response or at some special places in the service.

342. Face to Face

MRS. FRANK A. BRECK   Tune by GRANT COLFAX TULLAR

Mrs. Carrie E. Breck, who was married to Frank A. Breck in 1884, was a descendant of Colonel Timothy Ellis,

174

who became distinguished in the Battle of Ticonderoga in the American Revolution. She was a native of Vermont (January 22, 1855), lived for a while in Vineland, New Jersey, and then moved to Portland, Oregon. Five daughters were born to them, one of whom, Flora Elizabeth Breck, has written a number of hymns which have been published. Despite her many home cares, Mrs. Breck launched into the field of hymn-writing, her first success being "You ought to do something for Jesus," which appeared first in *The Christian Herald*. There have followed fifteen hundred hymns on various themes, none more popular than her "Face to face with Christ my Saviour."

Grant Colfax Tullar, who wrote the tune for this hymn, was born in Bolton, Connecticut, August 5, 1869. His parents died while he was an infant. His boyhood was a bitter struggle for existence. Converted at the age of nineteen, he entered Centenary Collegiate Institute at Hackettstown, New Jersey, and during this year developed his talents there in gospel hymns. He has preached and sung in evangelistic services all over this country, has written many gospel tunes, and in association with Isaac H. Meredith has published many Sunday school and evangelistic hymnals.

343. God Be with You Till We Meet Again

J. E. RANKIN   Tune by W. J. TOMER

The Rev. Dr. Jeremiah E. Rankin (1828-1904), who wrote "God be with you till we meet again," was a Congregational minister, serving pastorates in New England and other eastern states, and then becoming president of Howard University, Washington, D. C. He was the author of twelve volumes of prose and poetry, and edited the *Gospel Temperance Hymnal,* 1878. Of the writing of this hymn, he said:

Written in 1882 as a Christian good-by, it was called forth by no person or occasion, but was deliberately composed as a Christian hymn on the basis of the etymology of "good-by," which is "God be with you." The first stanza was written and sent to two composers—one of unusual note, the other wholly unknown and not thoroughly educated in music. I selected the composition of the latter, submitted it to J. W. Bishoff (the musical director of the little book we were preparing), who approved of it but made some criticisms which were adopted. It was sung for the first time one evening in the First Congregational Church in Washington, of which I was then the pastor and Mr. Bishoff the organist. I attributed its popularity in no little part to the music to which it was set. It was a wedding of words and music, at which it was my function to preside; but Mr. Tomer should have his full share of the family honor.

William Gould Tomer (1832-1896), a Civil War veteran, and a journalist, was teaching music in Washington at the time he composed this tune.

344. I Am Happy in the Service of the King

TUNE: *"In the Service of the King"*

A. H. ACKLEY   B. D. ACKLEY

During an evangelistic campaign in Wheeling, West Virginia, in 1912, one Sunday afternoon there was a meeting for men. B. D. Ackley, as he listened to the sermon (by "Billy" Sunday) became impressed with the idea that in spite of many struggles through which he had passed and was then passing, there was joy to him in the service of the King. With that thought came the musical theme for a song, which he at once jotted down and completed during the service. He sent the idea, "In the service of the King," and the melody to his brother, the Rev. A. H. Ackley, who wrote the words on this subject to fit the music. Not a single note of the music was afterwards changed from the melody, as it came originally to the composer, and while in the meeting it was given to him (as he afterwards said) like "transcribing from dictated phrases." (See No. 369.)

This is a wonderful song for young people because the great need in the world today is happy Christians, whose very happiness will be a recommendation of their religion. We need Christian young people to prove that it is possible to be happy and still be good.

345. I Love to Tell the Story

KATHERINE HANKEY   Tune by WILLIAM G. FISCHER

The daughter of an English banker, Miss Katherine Hankey, in 1866 wrote a long poem on the life of Jesus, in two parts. The first part was entitled "The Story Wanted," January 29, 1866, and the second part, "The Story Told," November 18, 1866. During the writing of the poem, Miss Hankey was taken seriously ill and much of its writing was accomplished while she was convalescing. From Part 2 were selected some of the stanzas to form the hymn, "I love to tell the story," which in this form has become immensely popular.

TUNE: The tune to this hymn was composed by William G. Fischer (see No. 358) at the request of Chaplain Charles C. McCabe, afterwards a bishop of the Methodist Episcopal Church, of which communion Fischer was an active member.

346.   I Shall See the King

W. C. POOLE   Tune by B. D. ACKLEY

The Rev. William A. Sunday, famous evangelist, has long held the hymn, "I shall see the King," to be one of his favorites for use in his revival meetings. He loves to lead the singing of this song, himself. When it is sung in his tabernacle, he takes off his coat and puts into the leading of this song all of his characteristic gestures.

The author of the hymn, the Rev. William C. Poole, is a Methodist pastor in the Wilmington (Delaware) Conference. His ancestors were Maryland Quakers, but his father and mother after their marriage became Methodists. Mr. Poole was born on a Maryland farm, was graduated from Washington College, and since entering the ministry has served Methodist pastorates in Delaware. In 1913 he was Superintendent of the Delaware Anti-Saloon League. He has written verses since he was in his twelfth year. Altogether he has written over five hundred hymns. He says:

My real work is that of a minister and pastor. The writing is done as recreation and diversion from responsibilities which might otherwise depress me. The same idea, which sends me to the pulpit, sends me to my pen or typewriter,—to help somebody.

The tune to this hymn was composed by B. D. Ackley in Philadelphia during a period of stressing "grind and hard work," as he has expressed it. (See No. 369.)

347. Some Day the Silver Cord

TUNE: *"Saved by Grace"*

FANNY J. CROSBY   GEORGE C. STEBBINS

When in 1891 Leander W. Munhall was conducting an evangelistic campaign in Newburgh, New York, he was associated with Mrs. Fanny J. Crosby Van Alstyne, the blind hymn-writer, and with George C. Stebbins, the singer and composer. One day there was a particularly beautiful sunset over the hills across the Hudson River, and Mr. Munhall described it to Fanny Crosby as best he could to one who had been blind since infancy. Suddenly she exclaimed: "Well, I cannot see the sunset that God has painted in the sky; but some day I shall see Him face to face." That gave to her a theme for the song that she wrote soon afterwards, "Some day the silver cord will break," with its chorus, "And I shall see Him face to face." George C. Stebbins set this to the music which ever since has been associated with it. (See Nos. 314 and 334.)

348. I Will Sing the Wondrous Story

F. H. ROWLEY   Tune by PETER P. BILHORN

F. H. Rowley wrote the song, "I will sing the wondrous story," in 1887 and brought it to Ira D. Sankey, who published it and popularized it by singing it in the D. L. Moody evangelistic meetings.

TUNE: Peter P. Bilhorn, who composed the popular tune to these words, was a well-known evangelist and gospel singer. (See No. 362.)

349. I'll Tell to All the World that God Is Love

TUNE: *"Till the Whole World Knows"*

A. H. ACKLEY   B. D. ACKLEY

Two brothers curiously collaborated in writing the words and music of the song, "I'll tell to all that God is love." They were the Rev. A. H. Ackley and B. D. Ackley. The latter tells the story in these words:

A. H. sent me this set of words with a melody. I had written a song with much the same sentiment. The verse of the one I had did not fit the idea I had worked out in the chorus. His chorus was not fitted to his verse melody. I simply took half of his and used it with my chorus, sending it out under my own name, of course; and then I used my verse with his chorus for another song and sent it to another publisher under his name. Really this song ("Till the Whole World Knows") and the other song mentioned are a combination affair. But it was all in the family. It made both songs what they should be, and no unfair advantage was taken in either case with the songs.

This has proved to be one of the most successful missionary messages among the gospel songs. (See No. 369.)

350. I've Reached the Land of Corn and Wine

TUNE: *"O Beulah Land"*

EDGAR PAGE STITES   JOHN R. SWENEY

Edgar Page Stites who wrote the song, "I've reached the land of corn and wine," was a native of Cape May County, New Jersey. On a visit to the Methodist campmeeting in Ocean Grove, New Jersey, he wrote this hymn, which was set to music by John R. Sweney, a song leader there; and it was first sung in one of the Ocean Grove meetings. When Mr. Sweney died in West Chester, Pennsylvania, his dear friend, Ira D. Sankey, sang this song at the funeral in the Methodist Episcopal Church, of which Mr. Sweney had been an active member. (See No. 320.)

351. In Sorrow I Wandered

TUNE: *"I Walk with the King"*

JAMES ROWE   B. D. ACKLEY

The composing of a tune to the hymn, "In sorrow I wandered," has a peculiar history. B. D. Ackley in June, 1911, had just finished his work in some meetings at Erie, Pennsylvania, and with his family he went to Winona Lake, Indiana, living in the home of Charles Allen, who in exchange took Mr. Ackley's house in Locust Street, Philadelphia, for the summer. The composer, Charles H. Gabriel, with his wife and son were guests of the Ackleys at Winona Lake for two weeks. One Sunday after the Tabernacle meeting, Mr. Ackley played over two tunes for Mr. Gabriel. The latter then suggested that he play

179

the verse of one and then the chorus of the other. The result was so striking that finally this new combination became the accepted tune for the song, "In sorrow I wandered" ("I Walk with the King"). Mr. Ackley has added to the incident these words about Mr. Gabriel:

What is true of this particular melody and suggestion has been true of his helpfulness to me in a musical way throughout the years. I sometimes wish it were possible for me to express in words what my heart feels toward this old friend. Our friendship of twenty-five years has never been marred by an unkind word, and my love for him is like that of a devoted son to a kind father. (See No. 369.)

I was singing this song for a large church, crowded full of colored folks in Philadelphia. As I finished the last stanza, a good old-fashioned type negro woman came down the aisle, her bonnet in one hand, the other raised in joyful rhythm; and she called out, "Hallelujah, Brudder, Ah walks wid Him too." Then, from all over the house came the response, "Yeh, we all walks wid Him down heah." And, after all, that is the real purpose of the song, to get folks to walk with Him.

352. Jesus May Come Today

TUNE: *"Is It the Crowning Day?"*

GEORGE WALKER WHITCOMB   CHARLES H. MARSH

"George Walker Whitcomb" is the *nom de plume* of the Rev. Henry Ostrom, one of the great Bible teachers in this country, who is in charge of the extension work of the Moody Bible Institute. George W. Sanville secured the song and its tune from Charles H. Marsh at Winona Lake, Indiana, for publication in the Rodeheaver gospel song books. It was first introduced into public use at the United Evangelical Conference at Allentown, Pennsylvania, in 1910.

353. Just a Few More Days

TUNE: *"Where the Gates Swing Outward Never"*

CHARLES H. GABRIEL   CHARLES H. GABRIEL

The words and music of "Just a few more days," here entitled "Where the Gates Swing Outward Never," were written by Charles H. Gabriel. His son, Charles H. Gabriel, Junior, was among the boys who went "over there" during the World War. The father came to New York to say "Good-bye" to him, and when the boy started for the army transport father and son put their arms about each other, and the boy said: "Dad, if I never see you again, I'll meet you where the gates never swing outward." With this message in his heart, Mr. Gabriel went back to the boy's mother in Chicago, and sat down and wrote this beautiful song, "Where the Gates Swing Outward Never." (See No. 330.)

354. Let the Song Go 'Round the Earth

SARAH G. STOCK   Tune by J. B. HERBERT

Sarah G. Stock's hymn, "Let the song go 'round the earth," was set to music by J. B. Herbert. (See No. 315.)

This is an exceptionally fine foreign missionary song, especially when it is linked with the idea that we could have a world-wide revival of religion with the gospel in song, if we had singers to take that gospel message around the world and sing it "with the spirit and the understanding." Young people of nearly every foreign field are interested in music, and could be attracted to our religion through music as in no other way.

355. My Days Are Gliding Swiftly By

DAVID NELSON   Tune by GEORGE F. ROOT

David Nelson was a surgeon in the United States Army in the War of 1812. Later he entered the ministry. While on a plantation in Missouri, he expressed his hatred of slavery too publicly, and was pursued by a mob who were bent on punishing him. He finally reached the banks of the Missouri River, opposite Quincy, Illinois, and signalled friends on the other side, who decided to rescue him when night came. Meanwhile, his pursuers came near to his hiding place, but could not find him. While he lay there in hiding, he wrote his hymn, "My days are gliding swiftly by," with its chorus, "For now we stand on Jordan's strand." When the darkness came, some mem-

bers of the Quincy Congregational Church in a canoe went
fishing near his hiding place and, watching their chance,
took him on board and ferried him across the river, pursued by the vengeful slaveholders. But he was safe in a
free State.

George F. Root has said this of the tune which he
composed for the hymn:

One day, I remember, as I was working at a set of graded part-
songs for singing classes, mother passed through the room and laid
a slip from one of the religious newspapers before me, saying:
"George, I think that would be good for music." I looked at the
poem, which began, "My days are gliding swiftly by," and a simple
melody sang itself in my mind as I read. I jotted it down and went
on with my work. That was the origin of the music of "The
Shining Shore." Later, when I took up the melody to harmonize it,
it seemed so very simple and commonplace that I hesitated about
setting the other parts to it. I finally decided that it might be useful
to somebody, and I completed it, though it was not printed until
some months afterward. In after years I examined it in an endeavor
to account for its great popularity—but in vain. To the musician
there is not one reason in melody or harmony, scientifically regarded,
for such a fact. To him hundreds of others, now forgotten, were
better.

356. Softly and Tenderly

WILL L. THOMPSON   Tune by WILL L. THOMPSON

The words and music of the invitation song, "Softly and
tenderly, Jesus is calling," with its appealing chorus,
"Come home, come home," were written by Will L. Thompson. He was a native of East Liverpool, Ohio (1849),
where he resided until his death in 1911, and a successful
business man and well-known song writer. While many
of his compositions were gospel songs, he composed also a
number of secular quartets, the best known of which is
"Come, where the lilies bloom."

357. Low in the Grave He Lay

ROBERT LOWRY   Tune by ROBERT LOWRY

Both the words and music of this Easter song were
written by the Rev. Dr. Robert Lowry, while he was pastor
of a Baptist Church in Brooklyn, New York. (See No.
287.)

358. Oh! Sometimes the Shadows Are Deep

E. Johnson   Tune by William G. Fischer

Though little is known about the author of the hymn, "Oh! sometimes the shadows are deep," E. Johnson, the musical setting was made by the composer of over two hundred hymn-tunes, William G. Fischer, a native of Baltimore, Maryland (October 14, 1835), and a well-known song-leader ever since his boyhood. He was professor of music at Girard College, Philadelphia, 1858 to 1868, and joined in the Moody and Sankey meetings in that city by leading a choir of one thousand voices. He died in 1912.

359. On Jordan's Stormy Banks I Stand

Samuel Stennett   Tune arranged from Dunham

The Rev. Samuel Stennett (1727-1824), a native of Exeter, England, was a Baptist minister, noted for his fine scholarship and spirituality. His famous hymn, "On Jordan's stormy banks I stand," was written for Rippon's *Selection* of hymns for public worship, 1787, and therein was entitled, "The Promised Land."

360. Saviour, Be with Me Every Hour

Charles H. Gabriel   Tune by Charles H. Gabriel

Both words and music of the hymn, "Saviour, be with me every hour," were written by the famous gospel song composer, Charles H. Gabriel, in 1924. It has been found to be very helpful as a prayer hymn. (See No. 330.)

Here is another simple song that choirs will find especially effective, if they will work out carefully the interpretation and use it in the proper places in the service. It is very fine to sing unaccompanied as a prayer response.

361. Sing Them Over Again to Me

Tune: *"Wonderful Words of Life"*

P. P. Bliss   P. P. Bliss

Philip Paul Bliss, born in Clearfield County, Pennsylvania, July 9, 1838, became one of the outstanding evangelistic singers and gospel hymn composers of his day. His education was limited. He early became a school teacher, the while studying especially in music. One of his earliest compositions he sold for a flute. Gradually he entered the work of singing at religious conventions, and after being in charge of the music at the First Congregational Church, Chicago, began evangelistic singing with Major D. W. Whittle, sometimes being associated with D. L. Moody. His gospel songs were widely used in the Moody meetings, among them being this hymn, "Sing them over again to me." He was on his way to sing in Mr. Moody's Tabernacle, Chicago, from his home in Rome, Pennsylvania, where he and his family had spent a happy Christmas, and was riding in a west-bound train, on December 29, 1876, when the bridge at Ashtabula, Ohio, gave way and the train crashed down sixty feet, killing both Mr. and Mrs. Bliss and many other passengers.

362. Sweet Peace, the Gift of God's Love

PETER P. BILHORN   Tune by PETER P. BILHORN

Peter P. Bilhorn, who wrote both words and music of the song, "Sweet peace, the gift of God's love," was born in Mendota, Illinois, 1861. His father was killed toward the end of the Civil War, and his boyhood was spent more in helping his widowed mother, than in education. When they moved to Chicago in 1876, the voice of this fifteen-year-old boy began to attract attention. He was converted in Moody's meetings in 1881, after hearing the evangelist preach on "Christ hath redeemed us," and at once he found the "Sweet peace," of which this song is so eloquent. He studied music under George F. Root and devoted his life to evangelistic singing and preaching.

363. We've a Story to Tell to the Nations

COLIN STERNE   Tune by H. ERNEST NICHOL

This rousing missionary hymn was written by an English contemporary poet and well-known composer, H.

Ernest Nichol, who has composed a great many tunes to his own hymns, the latter being attributed to his pseudonym, "Colin Sterne." Nichol was born December 10, 1862, in Hull, England, and received his degree of Mus. Bac. at Oxford in 1888. He has published fourteen festival services for Sunday school, containing 130 of his own tunes. "We've a story to tell to the nations" was written in 1896 and published in the *Sunday School Hymnary*, 1896.

364. What a Wonderful Change

Tune: *"Since Jesus Came into my Heart"*

R. H. McDaniel   Charles H. Gabriel

During the "Billy" Sunday campaign in Philadelphia, 1915, there was a policeman, assigned in the course of his duties to attend the meeting every night, who listened attentively to Mr. Sunday's sermons. But he steeled his heart against the message, until about two weeks before the end of the campaign, when Charles H. Gabriel, the composer, and I introduced the new song, "Since Jesus Came into my Heart." Learning the song along with the rest of the great audience the officer found that its melody and its message were more than he could resist. He yielded, and Jesus came in his heart through the power of song. The man was thoroughly converted, and during the two remaining weeks of the campaign he was the means of inducing more than a hundred other men to "hit the trail" and pledge their allegiance to Jesus.

I sang this song in Japan, having learned it phonetically in Japanese. At the conclusion of the song one night, a rickshaw puller came up to me and started talking to me excitedly in Japanese. The interpreter told me: "This man says that he was once a drunken rickshaw man and had no money and no rice. But he heard this song, and he let Jesus come into his heart. Now he has money and rice and over ten rickshaws, and he has men working for him." (See No. 330.)

365. Almost Persuaded

P. P. BLISS   Tune by P. P. BLISS

Evangelist Brundage was preaching on a passage from Acts 26, more particularly on the verse, "Almost thou persuadest me to be a Christian," and concluded his sermon with the striking sentence, "He who is almost persuaded is almost saved, and to be almost saved is to be entirely lost." Philip P. Bliss was in the audience and was so moved by the preacher's climax that he wrote the words and music of " 'Almost persuaded,' now to believe." (See No. 361.)

366. More Love to Thee, O Christ

ELIZABETH PRENTISS   Tune by WILLIAM H. DOANE

Mrs. Elizabeth Payson Prentiss (1818-1878) was the daughter of the famous Rev. Edward Payson of Portland, Maine. She married the Rev. Dr. George L. Prentiss, a Presbyterian clergyman and professor of Union Theological Seminary, New York city. In his *Life* of her, he tells the story of her hymn:

The hymn, "More Love to Thee, O Christ," belongs probably as far back as the year 1856. Like most of her hymns, it is simply a prayer put into the form of a verse. She wrote it so hastily that the last stanza was left incomplete, one line having been added in pencil when it was printed. She did not show it, not even to her husband, until many years after it was written; and she wondered not a little that, when published, it met with so much favor.

William H. Doane composed the tune. (See No. 307.)

367. Oh! Listen to Our Wondrous Story

TUNE: *"What Did He Do"*

J. M. GRAY   W. OWEN

The Rev. Dr. James M. Gray, author of the hymn, "Oh! listen to our wondrous story," is dean of the Moody Bible Institute in Chicago, Illinois. The melody to "What Did He Do" was written by W. Owen, the Welsh composer.

368. Upon a Wide and Stormy Sea
TUNE: "Sail On"
CHARLES H. GABRIEL   CHARLES H. GABRIEL

In 1909 the words and music of the song, "Sail On," were written by Charles H. Gabriel, the famous gospel song composer. (See No. 330.) When it was first printed, it did not have the additional ending, with the repetition of the phrase, "Sail on, sail on," etc. It was never successful until this effective climax was devised, and added to the song. But that little alteration made it especially popular with the great choruses which I led in the "Billy" Sunday evangelistic meetings.

Rehearse your choir carefully on this ending, and you will find it very effective. Have the basses and sopranos get a good breath before the very last phrase, and tenors and altos repeating the "Sail On," all gradually diminishing, then holding the very last tone of the faintest possible sound. You can also add to the effectiveness by teaching the chorus to the congregation and letting the very last "Sail on" come from the last seats in the gallery or back in the Sunday school room.

369. When the Night Is O'er
A. H. ACKLEY   Tune by B. D. ACKLEY

"When the night is o'er" is one of the many gospel songs in which the two brothers Ackley have collaborated, the Rev. A. H. Ackley writing the words and B. D. Ackley the music. The former was graduated from Westminster Theological Seminary, Maryland, when he was twenty-two years old, and became assistant pastor of the First Presbyterian Church, Sharon, Pennsylvania. He has served in a number of pastorates since then. He studied harmony and violoncello with Alfred Walker of the Royal Academy of Music, London. He began his hymn-writing in the spring of 1907, and has continued consistently writing ever since. B. D. Ackley was private secretary and pianist to the Rev. W. A. Sunday. He can play many different musical instruments, including the organ. He is a member of the Bethany Presbyterian Church, in Philadelphia.

370. Does Jesus Care

FRANK E. GRAEFF   Tune by J. LINCOLN HALL

The Rev. Frank E. Graeff has served as pastor of many churches in the Philadelphia Conference of the Methodist Episcopal Church. During that time he has written over two hundred hymns, as many stories, and a book, entitled *The Minister's Twins*. His most popular song, "Does Jesus care?" was produced during a period when he was pressed by deep anxieties and expressed his faith in Him when "burdens press and the cares distress." He has said of it, "The hymn seems to carry comfort and hope to troubled hearts, and I am glad I had the inspiration to write it."

The tune was composed by Dr. J. Lincoln Hall, a prominent Philadelphia song leader, gospel tune composer and music publisher. Born in that city, November 4, 1866, he was graduated with high honors from the University of Pennsylvania, thereafter continued higher studies in music, and received the degree of Mus. Doc. from Harriman University. His compositions include a Mass in D, cantatas and oratorios, as well as hundreds of Sunday school and gospel songs. In the latter field he has edited many hymnals.

371. Hover O'er Me, Holy Spirit

E. H. STOKES   Tune by JOHN R. SWENEY

The Rev. Dr. Elwood H. Stokes was for many years a pastor and presiding elder in the New Jersey Conference of the Methodist Episcopal Church. One of the founders of the religious community of Ocean Grove, New Jersey, he became the president of the Ocean Grove Association, which office he held until his death. At the holiness meetings in Thornley Chapel, there was felt the need of more hymns on the Holy Spirit, and in response to this feeling, Doctor Stokes wrote his hymn, "Hover o'er me, Holy Spirit." John R. Sweney, then song leader at Ocean Grove, being shown the hymn by its author, composed the tune; and, thus united, the words and music became a consecration hymn that was widely used in this country. (See No. 320.)

188

372. The World Is Bright, the World Is Good

CHARLES H. GABRIEL   Tune by CHARLES H. GABRIEL

"The world is bright, the world is good" is a hymn that was especially written in 1928 by Charles H. Gabriel, the gospel song composer, to help supply the need for the type of song which the religious education leaders of America have been seeking. (See No. 330.)

373. Father, Lead Me Day by Day

JOHN P. HOPPS   Tune by CHARLES H. GABRIEL

This is another hymn (*cf.* No. 372) composed to meet the special needs of present-day religious education. It was written in 1928.

374. My Hope Is Built on Nothing Less

EDWARD MOTE   Tune by WILLIAM B. BRADBURY

The Rev. Edward Mote (1797-1874), a native of London, England, was converted in 1813, after a godless youth, while listening to the preaching of the Rev. J. Hyatt, of Lady Huntingdon's Connexion, and joined the church under the Rev. Alexander Fletcher, two years later becoming a Baptist. In 1852 he left his trade as a cabinet-maker and entered the Baptist ministry, serving the church at Horsham, Essex, until his death in 1874. He edited *Hymns of Praise,* 1836, containing his hymn, "My hope is built on nothing less," which was first printed in a leaflet, 1834, and in the *Spiritual Magazine.* In his hymnal it bears the title, "The Immutable Basis of a Sinner's Hope." The author said of it: "One morning as I went to labor, it came into my mind to write a hymn on 'The Gracious Experience of a Christian.' As I went up Holborn I had the chorus,

> On Christ, the solid rock, I stand;
> All other ground is sinking sand.

In the day I had the first four verses completed and wrote them off." He sang these lines first to a friend who was dying, and, seeing the comfort this hymn imparted, he gave it to the world. William B. Bradbury composed our tune to this hymn. (See No. 325.)

375. He Leadeth Me

JOSEPH H. GILMORE   Tune by WILLIAM B. BRADBURY

The Rev. Joseph H. Gilmore, son of Governor Joseph A. Gilmore, of New Hampshire, was a native of Boston, Massachusetts (1834). After graduation from Boston University, 1854, and Newton Theological Seminary, 1861, he became pastor of the Baptist Church in Fisherville, New Hampshire, later pastor in Rochester, New York, and professor in Rochester Theological Seminary and the University of Rochester. In 1862 he was conducting a prayer-meeting in the First Baptist Church, Philadelphia, on the theme of the Twenty-third Psalm, and after the service in a home nearby continued the subject in conversation. He has told how the hymn grew out of this:

During the conversation, the blessedness of God's leadership so grew upon me that I took out my pencil, wrote the hymn just as it stands today, handed it to my wife, and thought no more about it. She sent it, without my knowledge, to the *Watchman and Reflector*. Three years later, I went to Rochester to preach for the Second Baptist Church. On entering the chapel I took up a hymn book, thinking: "I wonder what they sing." The book opened to "He Leadeth Me," and that was the first time I knew my hymn had found a place among the songs of the Church.

The popular tune to "He Leadeth Me" was composed by William B. Bradbury. (See No. 325.)

376. Jesus, I am Coming Home Today

A. H. ACKLEY   Tune by B. D. ACKLEY

B. D. Ackley tells the story of the hymn and tune, "Jesus, I am coming home today," in the following lines:

We had closed our meeting in Danville, Illinois, April, 1910, and our next meeting was at Bellingham, Washington. I realized that if I did not get home between these meetings, I would not see my youngest daughter, then not quite three months old, until the latter part of July. So I left the Danville campaign on Thursday before its close, and the train out of Terre Haute did not carry a parlor car.

I remember sitting in a stuffy day coach during a part of the ride. The click of the wheels over the rails was very noticeable, and I was soon humming along, keeping time with the clicks, using first one melody and then another, all without thought of composing a song—when the idea became fixed in my mind, "Well, I'm coming home today." It was a sort of telepathic message to the folks at home, that I was on my way.

This developed into the thought, "Jesus, I am coming home today." Taking out a little pad that I invariably carried with me in those days, I jotted down the idea and melody, suggested with the words and the beating of the cars upon the rails. I ran across that old pad last year (1929), and gave it to a friend of mine who wanted it as a keepsake. It had a rough draft of the song; in fact, the song as it now is, except a change or two, made later in one phrase of the chorus. My brother wrote the words to the melody I sent him, and I brought the song with me, when we opened the meetings at New Castle, Pennsylvania, in 1910.

This has proved to be a very effective invitation song in evangelistic meetings. Hundreds of people in the "Billy" Sunday campaigns have come forward down the aisle during the singing of this hymn in response to the evangelist's invitation to express their allegiance to Christ. Usually in these meetings, this song followed the singing of "Why Not Now?" (See No. 369.)

377. Wonderful Fountain that Cleanseth

E. E. HEWITT   Tune by B. D. ACKLEY

Miss Eliza Edmunds Hewitt wrote the words, and B. D. Ackley the music, of the song, "Wonderful fountain that cleanseth from sin"; both of them being at the time residents of Philadelphia. (See Nos. 320 and 369.)

INDEX